ANALECTA BIBLICA

INVESTIGATIONES SCIENTIFICAE IN RES BIBLICAS

104

A Prophet Confronts His People

The Disputation Speech in the Prophets

ROMAE
E PONTIFICIO INSTITUTO BIBLICO
1984

ADRIAN GRAFFY

ST. JOHN'S SEMINARY, WONERSH

A Prophet Confronts His People

The Disputation Speech in the Prophets

ROME
BIBLICAL INSTITUTE PRESS
1984

Vidimus et approbamus ad normam Statutorum Pontificii Instituti Biblici de Urbe

Romae
die 1 mensis iunii anni 1983

HORACIO SIMIAN YOFRE, S.I.
CHARLES CONROY, M.S.C.

ISBN 88-7653-104-1

PRINTED IN ITALY

TYPIS P.U.G. - ROMAE

*This book is gratefully dedicated
to my family and friends*

Preface

This work is a slightly expanded version of my doctoral dissertation, defended at the Pontifical Biblical Institute in April 1983. It is my pleasant duty to express deep gratitude to those who assisted me in the composition and publication of this study.

I offer my sincere thanks to the director of the thesis, Horacio Simian-Yofre S.J. He taught me to examine biblical texts with careful precision and guided my post-graduate studies with his friendly encouragement. My thanks are due also to Charles Conroy M.S.C., the second reader of the dissertation, for his scholarly advice and kindly guidance. I am grateful to Luis Alonso Schökel S.J. for accepting this study for the series Analecta Biblica, and to James Swetnam S.J., who oversaw the work of publication with his customary efficiency and dedication. I record my thanks to colleagues and friends in the Brentwood Diocese, who encouraged my academic progress and provided financial aid for this publication. This book is dedicated to my family and friends in deep appreciation of their constant support throughout the years.

Wonersh, September 1983   ADRIAN GRAFFY

Table of Contents

Abbreviations

AB	Anchor Bible
AnBib	Analecta biblica
AnOr	Analecta orientalia
AOAT	Alter Orient und Altes Testament
ATD	Das Alte Testament Deutsch
BBB	Bonner biblische Beiträge
BEvT	Beiträge zur evangelischen Theologie
Bib	*Biblica*
BibB	Biblische Beiträge
BibOr	Biblica et orientalia
BKAT	Biblischer Kommentar: Altes Testament
BWANT	Beiträge zur Wissenschaft vom Alten und Neuen Testament
BZAW	Beihefte zur *ZAW*
CAT	Commentaire de l'Ancien Testament
CBQ	*Catholic Biblical Quarterly*
DBSup	*Dictionnaire de la Bible, Supplément*
EBib	Etudes bibliques
EstBib	*Estudios biblicos*
EvT	*Evangelische Theologie*
FRLANT	Forschungen zur Religion und Literatur des Alten und Neuen Testaments
FzB	Forschung zur Bibel
GKC	*Gesenius' Hebrew Grammar*, ed. E. Kautzsch, tr. A. E. Cowley
HAT	Handbuch zum Alten Testament
HKAT	Handkommentar zum Alten Testament
IB	Interpreter's Bible
ICC	International Critical Commentary
IDB	G. A. Buttrick (ed.), *Interpreter's Dictionary of the Bible*
IDBSup	Supplementary volume to *IDB*
Int	*Interpretation*
JBL	*Journal of Biblical Literature*
KAT	E. Sellin (ed.), Kommentar zum A.T.
NTS	*New Testament Studies*
OBO	Orbis Biblicus et Orientalis
OTS	Oudtestamentische Studiën
RB	*Revue biblique*
RGG	*Religion in Geschichte und Gegenwart*
RSV	*Revised Standard Version*
SBLDS	Society of Biblical Literature Dissertation Series
SBT	Studies in Biblical Theology
TBü	Theologische Bücherei
THAT	E. Jenni and C. Westermann (eds.), *Theologisches Handwörterbuch zum Alten Testament*

TLZ	*Theologische Literaturzeitung*
TOB	*Traduction Oecuménique de la Bible*
TWAT	G. J. Botterweck and H. Ringgren (eds.), *Theologisches Wörterbuch zum Alten Testament*
TZ	*Theologische Zeitschrift*
VT	*Vetus Testamentum*
VTS	Vetus Testamentum Supplements
WMANT	Wissenschaftliche Monographien zum Alten und Neuen Testament
ZAW	*Zeitschrift für die alttestamentliche Wissenschaft*

A Prophet Confronts his People

One of the notable features of the speeches of the prophet Ezekiel is the frequency with which he reports what the people are saying and goes on to refute their opinion. Proud words of those left in Jerusalem receive unambiguous replies. Despondent laments of the exiles are answered by words of encouragement. This prophetic device, though common in Ezekiel, is by no means limited to him. This technique has often been given the name "disputation speech", but this term is used for other kinds of speech besides the clearly recognisable sequence of quotation of the people and refutation of their words. The designation is in fact used for many prophetic speeches which bear little resemblance to those displaying the technique concerned. Acceptable criteria for assigning a text to the genre "disputation speech" need to be found.

This study begins with a critical assessment of the way the disputation speech has been presented in genre study since the days of Hermann Gunkel. As the investigation proceeds it becomes apparent that the quotation-refutation pattern can provide the missing criterion for assigning a text to the genre.

The central part of the study presents all those prophetic speeches which use the device of refuting the quoted words of the people. Presentation of the texts as disputation speeches with an easily recognisable structure leads to a more accurate view of the extent of many speeches, a clearer grasp of their aim and a more precise interpretation of their message.

Once the major task of presenting the disputation speeches has been performed, a comment on the method used is pertinent. A comprehensive presentation of the elements of the genre is then provided. This considers both those elements found in all the disputation speeches, the introduction, quotation and refutation, as well as those found only in some of the texts, such as the programmatic refutation and the double refutation. Following this, the setting of the genre in the life of ancient Israel is described. Times of crisis required such a genre to allow the prophet to confront his people directly and correct their mistaken views. Finally, it is proposed that the NT too contains some examples of the genre in the preaching of Jesus.

Investigation of a technique perceived in the text of the OT leads to the elucidation of a genre mentioned with some frequency in OT study.

PART ONE

The Disputation Speech
in Genre Study

The most comprehensive account of the "disputation" is that of Hermann Gunkel, which he intended to be a programme for further study of the genre (Section 1). Studies of the disputation speech have proliferated above all in works on Deutero-Isaiah (Section 2), and to a lesser extent in studies of Malachi (Section 3). But disputation speeches have been sought out in other prophets too (Section 4).

1. Hermann Gunkel and other early contributors

A survey of the way the disputation speech has been presented must begin with the work of Hermann Gunkel. His fullest treatment of the prophetic material is found in his introductions to H. Schmidt's *Die grossen Propheten*[1]. In the final introduction Gunkel sets down a programme for the study of the genres found in the prophetic writings, which he sees as essential for the investigation of the history of the literature[2].

The disputation is the last of the genres to be presented by Gunkel[3]. It is not an adopted genre, but has its origin within prophecy as a result of differences of opinion between the prophet and his contemporaries. Disagreements with the people or even with other prophets had a marked effect on prophecy and influenced its modes of expression. Thus the disputation (*Streitgespräch*, *Disputation*) arose. To assist the reader to imagine such disputes Gunkel cites specific examples of situations where prophets found themselves in conflict with others[4].

Gunkel begins his examination of the disputation by describing the technique of quoting the opponents' words and refuting them. The prophet is obliged to counter objections raised against his message, and so devises the technique

---

[1] GUNKEL, Einleitungen, in SCHMIDT, *Die grossen Propheten*, xi-lxxii. Briefer though almost identical material is found in articles in *RGG*, ¹1913 and ²1930.
[2] GUNKEL, "Die Propheten als Schriftsteller und Dichter".
[3] GUNKEL, "Die Propheten als Schriftsteller und Dichter", lxix-lxxi.
[4] Amos 7,10ff; Isa 7; Jer 28; 1 Kgs 18,17ff; 22,24f.

of reporting the words of his opponents and refuting them, often powerfully and with passion. Gunkel gives as examples various texts from Amos to Haggai[5]. However, the passages cited are of various types.

It is unfortunate that the very first text given, Amos 5,14, only implies the people's words, and the prophet has no intention of refuting their conviction that God is with them. He exhorts them rather to behave in such a way that Yahweh may indeed be with them. In many of the examples Gunkel gives the quotations are not reported with a view to being refuted, but for other reasons, notably as part of an illustration of the guilt of the speakers which further justifies their coming punishment. In Isa 22,13 the words "let us eat and drink for tomorrow we will die" are part of a description of Jerusalem's uncaring attitude and failure to turn to Yahweh. Isa 28,9-10 contains a quotation attributed to the drunken priests and prophets of Jerusalem. Their derogatory remarks and mimicry of the prophet's speech are part of the accusation against them in vv.7-10. Not only do they spend their time in debauchery, but also directly insult God's prophet. Some of their remarks are taken up as part of the judgement in v.13. The role of the quotation in vv.9-10 is not to state an opinion to be refuted, but to give further weight to an accusation and further justification for a punishment. In Isa 28,15 the quotation of the leaders' words might be regarded as amounting to an accusation against them. Words of punishment will begin in v.17b. But when the quotation is understood as expressing an opinion which is then refuted all the elements of the reply, which begins in v.16, can be given their true value. Gunkel's view, that Isa 28,15 is the basis of a disputation speech, is to be accepted. In Isa 30,16, "no, we will flee on horseback! ... we will ride on swift chariots!" is much more clearly a quotation illustrating guilt than a view to be refuted. The same must be said of Zeph 1,12, "Yahweh does neither good nor evil", and of the texts from Jeremiah[6]. Although he names several verses in Jer 2, Gunkel omits mention of v.23a, where words attributed to Israel are indeed refuted. However, this half-verse cannot be considered a disputation speech because it is not an autonomous unit; it is part of the long poem in Jer 2 where rebellious words are repeatedly put on Israel's lips, as in vv.20a.25b.27.31b.35. The Ezekiel texts cited by Gunkel genuinely display the process of refutation of a quotation, with the exception of 21,5, which at the most is only implicitly refuted. Isa 40,27 is clearly a quotation later refuted, but the quotation in Isa 58,3 simply contributes to clarifying the people's attitude when fasting. Hag 1,2 is the only text of this prophet in which a quotation is refuted. Gunkel also describes Malachi as being made up almost exclusively of statement and counter-statement. Malachi in fact shows a quite different pro-

---

[5] Amos 5,14; Isa 22,12; 28,9ff; 28,14ff; 30,16; Zeph 1,12; Jer 2,20.25.27.35; 3,4f; 7,10; Ezek 11,3.15; 12,22f; 18,2; 21,5; Isa 40,27; 58,1ff; Hag 1,2; 2,3 and others.

[6] See the previous note.

cess from that of quotation followed by refutation, for it is God or the prophet who proposes the theme of the speeches with his own words.

Gunkel also notes that the quotations of the people given by the prophets are occasionally fictitious. This seems to be the case in Jer 7,10, where the words are again an illustration of guilt, but the quotation in Isa 28,15 can be considered quite true to life due to the arrogance of the rulers who speak it.

Gunkel maintains that differences of opinion between the prophets and others are the key to understanding many ideas of the prophets, even when a dispute is not presented explicitly. He gives as examples a series of texts in which no quotations of the opponents' words appear, some of which might equally well be considered to be unchallenged statements by the prophets, and not refutations of an opposing idea. Thus, in Amos 3,2, Gunkel sees an implicit disputation against the idea that Yahweh would never punish those he had chosen. The rhetorical question in Amos 9,7, seems to make it more likely that the people were indeed of a different opinion, considering themselves far superior to the Cushites, Philistines and Arameans. Amos 3,8, however, is not a refutation of the people's opinion, but rather an instruction on the compulsion the prophet feels to preach the message he receives. Isa 59,1-2 can be seen as an implicit refutation of the people's idea that Yahweh was unable to save them. But in all these instances, as Gunkel pointed out, the disputation is not explicit. It is only implied to some degree, if indeed it is present at all. In Isa 7,21-25 Gunkel sees a sinister interpretation of Israel's idea of the land as "flowing with milk and honey". They will eat curds and honey for there will be nothing else to eat. Similarly, Ezek 15 interprets for the worse the idea of Israel as the chosen vine. In these cases too the disputations are implicit. Finally, Gunkel sees a virtual disputation in the use of the expressions "do not rejoice, Israel!" and "unloved" in Hos 9,1 and 1,6. All these texts are at most implicit disputations, not expressly formulated. They cannot be assigned to the same genre as those texts where the clearly introduced quotation is followed by a refutation, for their structure is quite different.

In his final paragraph on prophetic disputations Gunkel stresses that it is above all the style of prophetic writing which changed due to the need to counter the objections raised against the prophets' teaching. Illustrative examples were thought up, parables devised and proverbs cited with the intention of convincing the people more forcefully. Amos 3,3-8 gives some analogies in the form of rhetorical questions in order to illustrate how the prophet felt compelled to utter his message. Amos 5,19, another implicit disputation, is cited here. Isa 5,1-7 and 28,23-29 are given as parables showing the disputation style, but the dominant tone of these units is not that of a disputation. The former announces judgement through a parable which leads to the self-condemnation of the listeners, and the latter gives another parable to instruct the people on the multifarious ways of God. Gunkel lists three uses of proverbs in a disputation style. In Ezek 12,22 the proverb is clearly quoted with a view to refutation in

the following verses. But the isolated proverb in Hos 4,11 simply adds to the
picture of Israel's guilt, and the proverb in Ezek 16,44 is by no means disputed.
Trial speeches in Deutero-Isaiah were another instance of this argumentative
style, as in 41,1ff.21ff; 43,9ff. Finally, Gunkel refers to the style of speech found
in Jer 2,14ff. and in Deutero-Isaiah generally.

It is evident that in this last paragraph of his treatment of the prophetic
disputation Gunkel has widened the horizon beyond even the implicit disputations to include other genres which basically seek to convince Israel of the prophets' message in a more argumentative tone. By introducing other genres
Gunkel seems to imply that what he presents as "disputation" is more comprehensive than one genre. He indicates the various devices used to impress the
listeners and convince them more forcefully. Most important in Gunkel's
presentation is the indication of the technique of the refutation of a quotation,
even though his examples were to some degree ill-chosen. Gunkel saw his treatment of the prophetic genres as an initial attempt to master an immense quanti-
ty of material[7]. The chief task as regards the disputation is to examine in detail
the process of the refutation of a quotation, which Gunkel gave pride of place in
his account.

Gunkel's collaborator, H. Gressmann, has little to say on the disputation
speech. He considers the *Diskussion* one of the less common genres of prophetic literature and gives Isa 28,7ff. and Jer 28 as examples of the polemical
background in which such discussions arose[8]. In his detailed examination of
Amos, Gressmann regards 5,18-20 as a "discussion", since he is unable to assign
it to another genre and Amos is plainly countering a false opinion[9]. But in a
later work he considers the same text a reproach *(Scheltwort)* which is at the
same time a polemic against false ideas[10].

E. Balla shows similar indecision when he describes Amos 3,1f.12; 5,18-20
and 6,12 as reproaches and threats arising from disputations, and considers
3,3-6.7.8 and 9,7 to have arisen in a similar way[11]. Both Gressmann and Balla
see the disputation as a product of the polemical activity of the prophet against
his opponents, but neither undertakes a detailed examination of the genre.

Before considering more substantial contributions to the debate on the
disputation speech brief reference should be made to the important study by H.
W. Wolff, "Das Zitat im Prophetenspruch". Wolff's main thesis in this exhaustive examination of the use of quotations by the prophets is that such
quotations illustrate guilt and form part of the motivation of coming
punishment[12]. The quotations in the disputation speeches, while representing a

---

[7] GUNKEL, "Die Propheten als Schriftsteller und Dichter", lxxii.
[8] GRESSMANN, *Die älteste*, 326.
[9] GRESSMANN, *Die älteste*, 347.
[10] GRESSMANN, *Der Messias*, 75.
[11] BALLA, "Amos", 309.
[12] WOLFF, "Das Zitat", 94-95. This study was first published in 1937 in *EvT* Beihefte.

challenge of some kind to the prophet and to God, cannot however all be said to reveal guilt. A quotation can express the people's sense of hopelessness, as in Ezek 37,11b and Isa 40,27.

2. Disputation Speeches in Deutero-Isaiah?

Deutero-Isaiah has received an inordinate amount of attention from form critics due to his novel use of form[13]. The resulting studies dedicate a great deal of space to the disputation speech in Deutero-Isaiah and tend to ignore its appearance in other prophets. The impression has been given that the genre of disputation speech is most prominent in Deutero-Isaiah, since a disproportionately large amount of bibliographical material on the disputation speech concerns this prophet.

L. Köhler gives a list of nine passages to which he gives the name *Streitgespräch*[14]. It can be seen from his presentation of the components of this genre, however, that he is dealing with what is commonly known as the trial speech.

J. Begrich follows Gunkel more closely in his treatment of the disputation speech[15]. He agrees with Gunkel that the genre is designed to win over the listeners and answer their objections, and provides some examples from other prophets[16]. The most common stylistic phenomenon in these texts is the rhetorical question, and only one passage, Jer 8,8, shows the structure of quotation followed by refutation. Begrich sees the disputation speeches of Deutero-Isaiah as a literary imitation of the controversies experienced by the prophet.

Begrich proposes two basic forms for the disputation speech. The first of these begins with a question which can perform one of two functions. In 40,18-20.25-26; 40,27-31 and 46,5-11 Begrich considers that the initial question serves to introduce the listener to the central point at issue in the dispute, while in 40,12-17 and 45,9-13 (which Begrich "corrects", partially according to the LXX) the opening questions bring about agreement on a parallel issue from which a consequence can be drawn regarding the central point of controversy. In 40,12-17 the opening questions are found in vv.12-14. These establish a basis of agreement between the prophet and his audience, from which certain

---

[13] GRESSMANN, "Die literarische Analyse", 295, considered that with Deutero-Isaiah the breaking-up of fixed prophetic genres began. MUILENBURG, *Isaiah 40-66*, 385, speaks of the frequent fusion of literary types in Deutero-Isaiah.

[14] KOEHLER, *Deuterojesaja*, 110-120.

[15] BEGRICH, *Studien*, 42-47.

[16] Amos 3,3-6.7-8; 9,7; Isa 10,8-11; 28,23-29; Jer 8,8; Malachi. Although Begrich mentions these texts (p. 42, n. 4) he undertakes no serious comparison of these speeches with his disputation speeches in Deutero-Isaiah. This objection to Begrich's work, namely that he works within the confines of one prophet, has been made again with regard to the priestly oracle of salvation by CONRAD, "Oracle of Salvation", 239.

preliminary statements follow in vv.15-16, leading into the decisive statement in v.17, against which no possible objection can be raised. It is questionable, however, whether the affirmation in v.17 shows any progress beyond vv.15-16. Thus in Begrich's analysis of this first form rhetorical questions are followed by statements of the central issue in a logical sequence of thought. Quite often, continues Begrich, this central issue is only implied and it is left to the people to deduce it, as happens in 40,19-20.26.

The second form of disputation speech is found most clearly in 44,24-28; 45, 18-21 and 48,12-15. These passages begin with a general statement that goes unchallenged. This is followed by a summons to the other party to gather and discuss the issue. Finally, the crucial point is reached and a rhetorical question invites the people to supply the intended answer. Begrich admits that in one of his three principal examples, 44,24-28, the summons is omitted, but he analyses the verses in such a way as to show a twofold passage from an initial accepted affirmation to a more controversial statement, and thus can assign this text to his second form. He notes that both here and elsewhere the prophet uses hymnic material to prove his point. (A full list of disputation speeches in Deutero-Isaiah according to Begrich is given in the table on pp.14-15.)

The essential feature of Begrich's disputation speech is a logical sequence of thought which passes from an initial question or statement to a controversial point. Begrich ignores the quotation and refutation structure given first place in Gunkel's account of the disputation. Begrich's disputation speech is fundamentally different in that its point of departure is a point of agreement, not a point of discord. The two processes seem to share only a common desire to convince the opposition. But, with Begrich, not only is the very point under discussion sometimes left unclear or implied, but even the very existence of a dispute between prophet and listeners is presumed on scanty evidence. The rhetorical questions often found here indicate rather the expected agreement of the listener. And even if one accepts, for example, that there is a progression in the argument between 40,15-16 and v.17, as Begrich proposes, it is still by no means proved that those hearing these words had taken a stand against the ideas here expressed. It is just as likely that they had no explicit opinion on the matter, or were even perfectly willing to assent to the prophet's every word. In short, to have a disputation speech, one ought to have a dispute. In many of Begrich's suggested texts the very presence of a disagreement is doubtful.

Furthermore, Begrich's disputation speeches admit of such variety of structure that one must question whether they can be assigned to one genre. Logical sequence of thought can indeed be traced; an earnest desire to convince a listener of a message (whether he is well-disposed or not) is certainly manifest; the stylistic device of the rhetorical question urges the listener's consensus; but a clear structure to underlie the genre is lacking. All there is here is a persuasive style of speaking which takes the listeners from a clearly agreed point to convince them of something which may be new to them.

H.-E. von Waldow takes a similar approach to the disputation speech in Deutero-Isaiah[17]. He reduces Begrich's forms to one basic structure: an agreed basis for discussion *(Disputationsbasis)* is followed by presentation of the contested point as a logical consequence of the first statement *(Schlussfolgerung)*. Like Begrich, von Waldow points out the frequent use of rhetorical questions to gain the people's assent in the first part of the structure. Like Begrich, he notes the use of well-known hymnic material to ensure agreement. Recollection of Yahweh's acts in creation or in salvation history, and descriptions of the worthlessness of idols also serve as points of unanimity to begin the disputation speeches. Thus the first part normally deals with well-known and accepted facts. On occasion, however, in the interests of clarity, the opposing opinion is cited, as in 40, 27, or a position is taken up against such an opinion, as in 55,8f. Thus the first part of von Waldow's disputation speech admits of a certain variety. The second part is even more varied, for it is adapted to the situation and subject of the controversy. Von Waldow describes the various points of style, and material characteristic of other genres used in this second part.

Von Waldow adds three passages to Begrich's list:44,21-22; 51,1-3 and 55,8-13. (For the full toll of the disputation speeches in Deutero-Isaiah according to von Waldow see the table on pp.14-15.) In contrast to Begrich he sees in 40,18-26 three incomplete disputation speeches and considers 45,9-11 a woe-oracle preceding a disputation. 50,1-3 is rejected completely and considered to be a judgement speech. This lack of agreement exposes the subjective nature of the criterion of logical sequence of thought proposed by Begrich and von Waldow for the genre. Von Waldow is critical of Begrich's analysis, and yet accepts its basic points. In contrast to Begrich, he considers the disputation speech to be an oral genre, and not a literary production. Like Begrich, von Waldow proposes a very loose structure for the disputation speech, and admits frequent irregularities and variations. His approach takes no account of the use of the disputation speech by other prophets. Is there anything more here than a vaguely definable sequence of thought? As with Begrich, the actual existence of a disagreement of opposing parties is merely presumed, and an opposing view is only rarely explicitly given. The thought sequence von Waldow suggests does not require the disagreement of the listener, which in a disputation speech ought to be explicit, or at least obviously implied in the text.

C. Westermann gives a brief account of the genre in his *Grundformen Prophetischer Rede*[18]. He considers the disputation speech *(Streitgespräch, Disputationswort)* to be one of the speech-forms borrowed by the prophets and states that this genre finds its proper form of expression in Deutero-Isaiah. Mic 2,6-11 is given as an example of the disputation speech. The passage does indeed contain a quotation of the people's words against the prophet in vv.6-7, but there is

---

[17] VON WALDOW, *Anlass und Hintergrund*, 28-36.
[18] WESTERMANN, *Grundformen*, 144-145.

no refutation of these words. As was apparent in many of the texts cited by Gunkel, and was amply illustrated by Wolff, the quotation here serves as an illustration of guilt, not as the opening statement in a dispute. Westermann does in fact note how close this text is to the judgement speech. Isa 28,23-29, the second principal example of a disputation speech cited by Westermann, is also to be rejected. It is a parable illustrating for the people the varied manner of God's dealings with Israel. Traces of disagreement on the part of the people are to be found nowhere in the text, and can at most be imagined as the background to it[19].

Westermann gives a fuller treatment of the disputation speech in his contribution to the debate on the genres in Deutero-Isaiah[20]. He questions whether one should speak of the disputation speech as a genre since Begrich's texts show such variety. He thus refers to it as a "speech-form" *(Redeform)*. The principal reason for Westermann's scepticism about the existence of a genre here is the lack of a clear common structure, but in demoting the disputation speech to the rank of a speech-form he seems to be yielding to Begrich's view without investigating the possibility of a more clearly structured genre.

Westermann proposes that this speech-form should not be called *Disputationswort*, but rather *Bestreitung*. In this way he means to draw a clear distinction between disputations in which the dialogue of the two opposing sides is exactly reported in direct speech (which he calls *Streitgespräch* or *Disputation*), and disputations in which the opposition's opinion is reported by the speaker (which he calls *Bestreitung*). It seems unnecessary to introduce a further term into a field already choked by an overgrowth of terminology, and better to use the term "disputation" or "dialogue disputation" *(Streitgespräch, Disputation)* as a genre designation for the dialogue reporting such a controversy, and "disputation speech" *(Disputationswort)* for the genre in which only the prophet speaks and reports the opposing viewpoint himself. This distinction is useful also beyond the prophetic literature. The term "disputation" *(Streitgespräch, Disputation)* is commonly used for a variety of other material. Westermann refers elsewhere to disputations in Egyptian and Babylonian literary traditions, and in the book of Job[21]. The term *Streitgespräch* is also used generally in the NT for argumentative dialogues between Jesus and his adversaries[22]. All these speeches, in Egyptian and Babylonian literature, in Job and in the NT, can suitably be called "disputations" or "dialogue disputations". The term

---

[19] WESTERMANN, *Grundformen*, 145, also lists Jer 2,23-25; 2,29-30.34-35; 8,8-9.
[20] WESTERMANN, "Sprache und Struktur", 124-134.
[21] WESTERMANN, *"Streitgespräch"*, 1883. In *Hiob* he describes the *Streitrede* as a comprehensive form which embraces all those forms which can be used to take up one position against another. MURPHY, *Wisdom Literature*, 175-176, similarly describes the disputation as an "overarching" genre. The book of Job also contains two small sections which might be considered disputation speeches, in the speeches of Elihu: Job 33,8-12 and 34,5-9.
[22] REICKE, "Streitgespräch", 1883-1884, gives a full list of NT disputations.

"disputation speech" is to be reserved for those speeches in which the speaker himself reports the opposing view and goes on to refute it.

Westermann maintains that the disputation speeches of Deutero-Isaiah mark the mid-point in the development of this speech-form, which finds final expression in Malachi[23]. He notes particularly the inadequate grounds for considering Isa 44,24-28 to be a disputation speech. The question in the corrected reading of v.24 is rhetorical, therefore presuming the agreement of the hearer, and thus cannot be considered a challenge to an opposing viewpoint. Westermann then introduces 49,14-15, a text omitted in the work of Begrich and von Waldow on disputation speeches, which according to any reasonable criteria is a suitable candidate for the genre. Indeed, 49,14-15 and 40,27-31 are the only two specimens of clear answers to explicit objections to be found in Deutero-Isaiah. In Westermann's view they are both parts of larger compositions, 49,14-26 and 40,12-31. These compositions have an important place in the structure of Isa 40-55, standing at the beginning of the two halves of the book[24]. Westermann gives a detailed analysis of these two texts. The implication is that they are disputation speeches because they provide an answer to an explicit objection. The logical conclusion of Westermann's work would be to propose that the clear statement of an opposing viewpoint followed by its refutation is the basic structure of the disputation speech. These two texts are not pure examples of the genre. Deutero-Isaiah is extremely free in his adaptation of the genre, bringing in elements of praise of God in 40,12-31 and in 49,14-26 elements of the lament[25]. What is lacking in Westermann's presentation is a detailed comparison of the disputation speeches he sees in Deutero-Isaiah as free developments of the genre with the stricter uses of the genre in other prophets.

Investigation concerning the disputation speech in Deutero-Isaiah continues with the work of H.-J. Hermisson[26]. He gives no explanation of his preference for the term *Diskussionswort*. Like Westermann, he doubts that there really is a genre here due to the great variety in the texts usually proposed. The lack of a clear *Sitz im Leben* is also a serious difficulty. Referring to Ezek 12,26-28 and Amos 3,3-6.8 he states that the common element is neither the quotation, nor the presence of reasoned argument, but an intention to correct the people's opinion. (One may question whether this is indeed present in Amos 3,3-6.8.) This intention is not expressed in specific forms and therefore talk of a genre is not justified. The greater part of Hermisson's article is

---

[23] WESTERMANN, "Sprache und Struktur", 125-126.

[24] Thus also WESTERMANN, *Jesaja*, 26.

[25] WESTERMANN, *Jesaja*, 18, also lists *Anklänge* of the disputation speech in 45,11-13; 45,18-19; ch. 46; ch. 48; 55,8. Westermann's uncertainty is betrayed in his conclusion on 40,12-31, where he states the passage to be a compilation of four disputations, but that only the last of them, vv.27-31, is the real disputation (p. 53).

[26] HERMISSON, "Diskussionsworte", 665-680.

dedicated to challenging von Waldow's proposals. Hermisson states that von Waldow is merely proposing a common logical form of thought, and questions whether this form of thought of *Disputationsbasis* followed by *Schlussfolgerung* does in fact exist in the texts. After a close examination of Isa 40,12-31; 40,27-31 and 44,24-28a Hermisson comes to the conclusion that the two-part structure is a fiction. Agreement of speaker and listeners cannot always be taken for granted in the so-called *Disputationsbasis*, as is apparent in 40,27-31, nor can progress from a known fact to a new element always be proved, as in 40,27-31. Deutero-Isaiah intends to confront scepticism, but not with the method suggested by von Waldow. Rather, he takes the listeners with him along a path on which decisions are constantly to be made. There is thus no genre of disputation speech in Deutero-Isaiah, but rather a common purpose approached with frequently recurring stylistic devices, such as quotations and questions, to convince the people of the message of salvation entrusted to the prophet.

Hermisson's article exposes the implicit nature of von Waldow's structure, where so much is left to the subjective judgement of the investigator. But Hermisson makes no attempt to find an alternative structure for the genre disputation speech. He speaks rather of the similar function of these texts to confront the hearers, which leads him to bring them together under the common designation "discussion speeches". He recognises that they cannot be considered as constituting a genre.

In spite of the criticisms of von Waldow's structure by Westermann and Hermisson, A. Schoors maintains that von Waldow has "exactly grasped" the structure of the disputation speech in Deutero-Isaiah[27]. Despite this apparent agreement he does not accept three of von Waldow's disputation speeches, implying how subjective the criteria followed are. (The table on pp.14-15 gives the full list of disputation speeches in Deutero-Isaiah according to Schoors.) He proposes 40,12-31 as the first disputation speech, but is unsure whether vv.12-26 are really intended as a "substructure" for vv.27-31[28]. The starting-point for all Deutero-Isaiah's disputation speeches in Schoors' opinion is the idea of Yahweh as creator, or as master of history, or both. The conclusion is that Yahweh is able to save his people. The role of Cyrus is often prominent in this second part. Schoors concludes that "the analysis given above points to a genre clearly characterized in form and content"[29]. In fact, the content has been summarised in such general terms as to be applicable to most of Isa 40-55, and the forms in the texts treated show such wide variety that it is hard to see how they can be considered characteristic of a genre. Once again, a serious flaw is the fact that no comparison is attempted with disputation speeches beyond Deutero-Isaiah.

---

[27] SCHOORS, *God your Saviour*, 245-295. Schoors gives his explicit approval of von Waldow's structure on p. 295.

[28] SCHOORS, *God your Saviour*, 259.

[29] SCHOORS, *God your Saviour*, 295.

R. F. Melugin, on the other hand, rejects von Waldow's structure as inadequate[30]. He sees several forms of disputation speech in Deutero-Isaiah and stresses the prophet's free use of other literary forms in his disputation speeches. The texts are "free creations" of Deutero-Isaiah and show great variety. Isa 40,12-17 displays the characteristics of the wisdom disputation found in Job 40,25ff. Isa 40,18-24.25-26 and 46,5-11 have a common structure which is Deutero-Isaiah's own creation. Isa 40,27-31 shows the style of psalms of lamentation with an expression of confidence in the reply. Isa 45,9-13 is designated by Melugin a "handler-handled" disputation and parallels are cited in Isa 10,15; Isa 29,15-16 and Rom 9,20ff. It is surprising that Isa 49,14-26 is not accepted considering the variety shown in the other examples. In fact this great disparity shows the impact of various traditional genres. One cannot speak of one structure in the disputation speech as von Waldow does. Melugin concludes: "But even here the utterances are disputations throughout and in this sense can be distinguished from their context by form."[31] He does not explain, however, how they can be so distinguished. Perhaps this distinction is conditioned by being traditionally described as disputation speeches. Melugin shows that the various texts usually proposed as disputation speeches in fact have formal elements in common with other texts, but not among themselves. Thus the texts proposed do not constitute a genre, but rather show a common disputing style.

K. Elliger's commentary on Deutero-Isaiah, though it covers little more than the first five chapters of the prophet, nevertheless makes his position as regards the disputation speech quite clear. The aim of the disputation speech is either to stress one's own position, or to expose the fallacy of the opposition, but the structure is that laid down by von Waldow: from a generally accepted basis the desired conclusion is drawn[32]. Elliger considers Westermann's presentation of 40,12-31 to betray a narrow idea of the disputation speech, in which a clearly expressed opinion is contested. He regards this as one type of the genre. But besides this there is another type, not directly contesting another's view, but setting out to defend an opinion on which doubts have been expressed[33]. An example of this is 40,12-17, which he treats as a separate disputation, the consequence being expressed in v.17, in accordance with von Waldow's structure. Elliger goes some way towards admitting that the opposing view is not clear, but still considers it essential to the disputation speech and therefore necessarily present in the text. In fact, the text of vv.12-17 by no means demands a difference of opinion between prophet and listeners. 40,18-26 (omitting vv.19-20) is regarded as the second disputation speech. It is a free adaptation of the basic schema, where the conclusion is expressed implicitly by

---

[30] MELUGIN, *Isaiah 40-55*, 28-44. In his earlier "Deutero-Isaiah and Form Criticism", 326-337, he had considered Isa 40,12-31 as a test case.

[31] MELUGIN, *Isaiah 40-55*, 44.

[32] ELLIGER, *Deuterojesaja*, 44.

[33] ELLIGER, *Deuterojesaja*, 46.

the imperative in v.26[34]. Elliger forces von Waldow's structure upon 40,27-31. V.27b is reduced to a "starting-point" (*Einsatzpunkt*), and Elliger has some doubts as to how to apply von Waldow's structure to vv.28-31, finally dividing the basis in vv.28-29 from a conclusion in vv.30-31[35]. In fact, the primary division in the text is that of the quotation in v.27 and the response to it in vv.28-31.

Elliger shows how widely applicable von Waldow's structure is by applying it to a new text, 42,5-9, which he regards as a disputation speech containing the oracle of the call of Cyrus. The main point of the text, the call of Cyrus in vv.6-7, is inserted as a foreign body between the two parts of the structure, the basis in v.5 and the "real disputation speech" in vv.8-9[36]. Finally, Elliger rejects the widely accepted text, 44,24-28, considering it primarily an address of Yahweh the king to the heavenly court, as in 42,1-4, though conceding that it shows traits of the salvation oracle and disputation speech[37].

Thus Elliger follows by and large the basic structure suggested by von Waldow, and displays by his choice of texts, even in the limited range of the first five chapters of Deutero-Isaiah, just how widely the structure can be applied. It is abundantly clear by now that what is presented here is a logical progression of thought, so generic as to be hard to apply with rigour, and which does not show any clear structure.

R. P. Merendino limits his study to Isa 40-48. He describes the disputation speech as a speech in which Yahweh responds to an objection which questions his power in the face of a specific circumstance[38]. The disputation speech thus serves to make the listeners aware of Yahweh's power in history. Merendino sees as conforming to such a description 40,27-31; 41,1-4, which at first sight might seem a judgement speech; and 42,5-9[39]. He also presents other texts as disputation speeches in part[40]. Merendino does not consider the question of the structure of the disputation speech as such. His definition is based on the content of texts which demonstrate Yahweh's power in history.

A final contribution to the discussion of the nature of the disputation speech in Deutero-Isaiah is made by B. D. Naidoff. In an analysis of Isa 40,12-31 he raises the question of the structure of the disputation speech in Deutero-Isaiah[41]. In spite of Hermisson's objections, Naidoff still considers von

---

[34] ELLIGER, *Deuterojesaja*, 69.

[35] ELLIGER, *Deuterojesaja*, 94.

[36] ELLIGER, *Deuterojesaja*, 228-229.

[37] ELLIGER, *Deuterojesaja*, 465.

[38] MERENDINO, *Der Erste*, 326.

[39] MERENDINO, *Der Erste*, 118, 128, 251.

[40] On p. 208 41,21-29 is considered a judgement speech which contains a disputation speech. On p. 327 Merendino contrasts the disputation speech with the judgement speech. He describes material within 42,19-24 as both disputation speech and warning *(Mahnwort)*. A similar description is given to 43,22.26-28. In his detailed treatment of the same speeches, on pp. 286 and 354-356 respectively, he had called both only warnings. On p. 327 too 45,18-19 is called a disputation speech. Later, on p. 451, it will be described as "more than a disputation speech".

[41] NAIDOFF, "Isaiah 40,12-31". 62-76.

Waldow's division of "basis" and "conclusion" to be useful. But he adds two qualifications to von Waldow's analysis. He admits that the progression of thought is not always readily apparent, and proposes that a third element, the "statement of the issue", begins the argument. He concedes, however, that this element is absent in 40,12-17 and 44,24-28. In a further article, considering Isa 45,9-13, Naidoff proposes that the structure of basis and conclusion is present twice, and regards v.11 as both the conclusion of the first disputation and the "statement of issue" of the second[42]. This shows how the "structure", which amounts really to a logical process of thought, can be applied with great abandon. Naidoff does not face up to Hermisson's attack on von Waldow's structure. And in Naidoff's work there is again no comparison with disputation speeches outside Deutero-Isaiah.

The disputation speech as commonly understood in Deutero-Isaiah has become something far removed from what Gunkel envisaged. He considered the speech as arising from differences of opinion between the prophet and his contemporaries. The disputation speech interpreted as a logical process of thought passing from basis to conclusion, with no clear indication whether the listener agrees or not, does not merit the title "disputation speech".

The following table illustrates the variety of texts from Deutero-Isaiah presented as disputation speeches.

Proposed Disputation Speeches in Deutero-Isaiah

	Begrich	von Waldow	Westermann	Schoors	Melugin	Elliger	Merendino
40,12-17	X	X			X	X	
40,18-20	X	Fragment					
40,25-26	X	Fragment	X	X	X	X	
40,21-24	Fragment	Fragment					
40,27-31	X	X			X	X	X
41,1-4							X
42,5-9						X	X
42,18-25					X		
44,21-22		X					
44,24-28	X	X		X	X	======	
45,9-13	X	vv.11-13		X	X		

---

[42] NAIDOFF, "Isaiah 45,9-13", 180-185.

	Begrich	von Waldow	Westermann	Schoors	Melugin	Elliger	Merendino
45,18-25	X	X					
46,5-11	X	X		X	X		
48,1-11	X	X		X	X		
48,12-15	X	X		X			= = = = = =
49,14-26			X				
50,1-3	X						
51,1-3		X					
55,8-13		X		X			

3. **Disputation Speeches in Malachi?**

Although the prophecies of Deutero-Isaiah have been the object of most of the research concerning the disputation speech, other prophets have received some attention. The only other detailed studies in an individual prophet concern the book of Malachi.

E. Pfeiffer notes the lack of accord on the nature of the material in Malachi, in spite of what he regards as Gunkel's clear lead[43]. The disputation speeches in Malachi are, in Pfeiffer's view, part of a long tradition of disputation speeches. He gives Amos 5,18-20 as a first example, but describes it as an "implicit disputation speech" because the words of the people are not given. Isa 40,27-31 is presented as a true disputation speech, and Pfeiffer adopts von Waldow's structure of "basis" and "conclusion". He also mentions in passing the disputation speeches of Ezekiel.

Though he pays lip-service to von Waldow's structure, Pfeiffer implies that what happens in a disputation speech is that an opinion of the people, clearly stated, is rejected, for this is what happens in Isa 40,27-31 and the Ezekiel texts he cites[44]. It is therefore all the more surprising that Pfeiffer considers the speeches found in Malachi to be disputation speeches.

Pfeiffer proposes the six speeches to be 1,2-5; 1,6 - 2,9; 2,10-16; 2,17 - 3,5; 3,6-12 and 3,13-21. He rejects 3,22-24 and 2,11-12 as secondary. In each of these six speeches Pfeiffer rightly sees an identical three-part structure. Each speech begins with a "statement" (*Behauptung*) by Yahweh (1,2a; 1,6; 3,6-7a; 3,13a) or by the prophet (2,10.13; 2,17a). This "statement" can take various forms: it can

---

[43] PFEIFFER, "Disputationsworte", 546-568.

[44] PFEIFFER, "Disputationsworte", 553. The Ezekiel texts in question are those proposed by W. Zimmerli. See below p. 20, n. 64.

be a genuine statement, as in 3,13, but it can also be a question, as in 2,10. In 3,7 it ends in an imperative. The second element is the "objection" (*Einrede*), which takes the form of short questions, asking for further clarification (1,2a; 1,6b; 2,14a; 2,17a; 3,7b; 3,13b). A second "objection" is found in 1,7a in the second speech, and in 3,8a in the fifth. The third stage, sometimes called "explanation" (*Begründung*), is the remaining part of each speech and clarifies the opening statement, leading to a conclusion.

Pfeiffer's analysis of the structure of the speeches in Malachi is essentially sound. But this structure is particular to Malachi, and quite different from that found in Isa 40,27-31, Pfeiffer's principal example of the disputation speech. In that text words of the people were quoted and then countered. In the speeches of Malachi, by contrast, the opening words are of God or the prophet, not of the people. The fundamental difference is that the aim of the forms in Malachi is to convince the listeners of the initial stated point, and not to reject the people's quoted opinion.

Pfeiffer maintains that Malachi shows a legitimate development of the genre, a late form of the disputation speech, which differs only quantitatively, not qualitatively, from other disputation speeches. It must be stated that after giving detailed attention to the structure of the six speeches Pfeiffer throws overboard the logical conclusion. His chief criterion for assigning a text to a genre is not in fact the structure, in spite of appearances, but rather the tone of the speeches, the fact that a certain resistance may be seen in the questioning of the prophet by the people. In fact, the primary aim of the speeches of Malachi is not to contest the people's views. There is indeed a qualitative difference between the disputation speeches which have precisely this aim and the forms found in Malachi. Malachi does provide two quotations of the people longer than the brief questions constituting the "objections". The people express their opinion that Yahweh favours the wicked in 2,17b during the fourth speech and that it is consequently useless to serve Yahweh in 3,14-15 during the sixth. Such expression of an opinion which is then refuted might suggest a true disputation speech. But the function of the quotations in these two cases is different. They come in the third part of the structure as part of the explanation of the opening statements in 2,17a and 3,13a respectively.

Pfeiffer's work on Malachi is praised by H. J. Boecker[45]. He proposes, however, two changes of terminology for the description of the speeches. The opening words of each speech should not be described as the "statement" (*Behauptung*) but as the "opening sentence of the discussion" (*Satz der Gesprächseröffnung*). This objection is fully justified, considering the opening "statement" is on one occasion a question (2,10). Boecker then considers how the two designations "disputation speech" (*Disputationswort*) and "discussion speech" (*Diskussionswort*) are used with no accepted differentiation. Boecker

---

[45] BOECKER, "Bemerkungen", 78-80.

prefers the latter designation for Malachi's speeches (*Diskussionsworte* or *Streitgespräche*). In this short article Boecker touches on the problem, that in fact the primary aim is not to dispute a statement, but he contents himself with remarks concerning the terminology.

G. Wallis accepts both Pfeiffer's analysis and Boecker's refining of the terminology[46]. He asserts that the discussions do not give an account of actual arguments but have their origins in them. Wallis proposes that 1,6 - 2,9 and 3,1-4 were originally directed to the priests, while the rest of the book was for lay-people. In both the part directed to the priests and that directed to the lay-people he sees a progression from accusation, to threat, to promise of salvation. But, contrary to what Wallis maintains, 3,1-4 is not a salvation speech and gives more accent to the coming judgement, and it is not necessarily directed to the priests. Wallis' distribution of the material to two original audiences is un-proven. The part clearly directed to the priests, 1,6 - 2,9, simply forms one of the six speeches.

J. A. Fischer speaks of a "catechetical" emphasis in Malachi and gives im-portance to the questions and responses by Yahweh in the speeches[47]. Unfor-tunately, he does not know of the work of Pfeiffer and has nothing to say of the literary genre of disputation speech.

4. Other contributions to the study of the Disputation Speech

The disputations found by H. W. Wolff in Amos all have the aim of convinc-ing the hearers of the inevitability of the coming judgement[48]. The three texts Wolff mentions, Amos 3,3-6.8; 5,18-20 and 9,7, each have quite different struc-tures. Amos 3,3-6.8 is a series of nine rhetorical questions showing various ex-amples of cause and effect, culminating in Yahweh's command which impels the prophet to speak. Wolff calls this a "learned disputation" (*lehrhafte Disputa-tion*)[49]. Amos 5,18-20 is described as a splendid example of prophetic ingenuity: the "framework genre" (*Rahmengattung*) is the woe-oracle, a "component genre" (*Gliedgattung*) of didactic questions is inserted, and a short narrative is added as an illustration (*Vergleichsstück*)[50]. Amos 9,7-10 is regarded as a discussion because it displays the style of a disputation[51]. The common characteristic of these three texts is their argumentative tone aiming to con-vince the hearers, but the only similarity of structure is the rhetorical question (3,3-6.8; 5,18b.20; 9,7). There is no quotation of an opposing point of view held

---

[46] WALLIS, "Wesen und Struktur", 229-237.
[47] FISCHER, "Notes", 315-320.
[48] WOLFF, *Amos*, 119.
[49] WOLFF, *Amos*, 220.
[50] WOLFF, *Amos*, 299.
[51] WOLFF, *Amos*, 396-397.

by the people addressed, except in 9,10b. But the function of this quotation is rather to give a further reason why they should indeed perish by the sword. Otherwise, such a contrasting opinion is implied in 5,18-20, but quite absent from 3,3-6.8. In his commentary on Hosea, Wolff speaks generally of a "disputation style", characterised by reference to Yahweh in the third person. It is found in 4,10-15; 8,11-13 and 12,1-15, among other texts[52]. The passages which he cites have no structural similarities, nor do they intend to contest a clearly expressed contrary opinion.

K. Koch proposes two types of disputation speech (*Diskussionswort*) in Amos, those of the prophet and those of God. He accepts Amos 3,3-8 as a disputation speech of the prophet[53]. He tentatively proposes that 3,12, which Wolff had rejected as a disputation speech due to the messenger formula, is a disputation speech of God[54]. It is hard to see the necessary background of disagreement to this verse. Koch describes 9,7 too as a disputation speech of God[55]. These three examples have no common structure, and the difference of opinion is again conjectured.

Wolff's analysis of Amos 5,18-20 is criticised by C. Hardmeier, who deals in passing with the disputation speech as one genre introduced by *hôy*, part of his demonstration that *hôy* is not a sign of a specific genre[56]. For Hardmeier Wolff's analysis of Amos 5,18-20, which speaks of woe-oracle, didactic questions and narrative, illustrates the tendency to identify form and genre. Having analysed this same text Hardmeier proposes that the elements essential for the disputation speech are the presence of two parties with contrasting opinions, the statement of the opinion to be contested and the correction of that opinion, however this comes about[57]. Hardmeier thus describes accurately the function or aim of the disputation speech.

He goes on to give further examples, continuing his attempt to show that *hôy* can introduce disputation speeches. The first of these, Isa 1,4-9, does not fulfil Hardmeier's own condition that a contrary view be corrected, for the question in v.5 does not reveal a contrary opinion, as Hardmeier maintains. Isa 10,5-15 does convey a contrast of opinions in that Assyria considers itself a power free to destroy rather than Yahweh's instrument for punishment. The argument of Assyria is rejected by rhetorical questions in v.15. In Isa 29,15-16 the question of the people in v.15b betrays their rebellious attitude, which is rejected in v.16 with rhetorical questions, as in 10,15. In Isa 45,9-13 the attitude of the opponents is again implied to be one of rebellious independence from God. This attitude too is refuted by the rhetorical question in v.9b. Thus Amos

---

[52] WOLFF, *Hosea*, xiv-xv.
[53] KOCH, *Amos*, I, 128-131.
[54] KOCH, *Amos*, I, 134-135, and II, 20.
[55] KOCH, *Amos*, I, 232-233.
[56] HARDMEIER, *Texttheorie*, 269-275.
[57] HARDMEIER, *Texttheorie*, 271, n.23.

5,18-20; Isa 10,5-15; 29,15-16 and 45,9-13 conform to the description Hardmeier lays down for the disputation speech, for their intention is to reject mistaken attitudes. They also have the similarity of beginning with *hôy* and that rhetorical questions are used to refute the contested opinion (Amos 5,20; Isa 10,15; 29,16; 45,9b)[58].

However, these texts do not begin with a formal statement of the opponent's opinion, as found when a formally introduced quotation of the opponent's words is then refuted. Hardmeier's description of the function of the disputation speech is applicable to such units too, but he considers no texts showing this structure, since none is introduced by *hôy*. In fact, Hardmeier's description, while adequately describing the function of those units showing the quotation and refutation structure, is not adequate to describe the function of the texts he himself presents. The *hôy* which introduces all of them gives an added threatening tone to the units, which is relevant to a description of their function. *hôy* may not indeed determine the genre and may be best described as a stylistic device to open the unit with a call to attention, but the use of *hôy* has a sure effect on the function of these units in that it constitutes a threat to those whose attitude is being challenged. Hardmeier himself maintains that the use of *hôy* brings with it associations of lament for the dead or for a disaster[59]. The use of *hôy* to open a speech is an indirect indication of bad news[60]. In Amos 5,18-20 the implicit announcement of disaster justifies the presence of *hôy* as the opening of the speech. In Isa 10,5-15 and 29,15-16 the *hôy* suggests the disastrous consequences of the ideas put forward by Assyria and by the people. *hôy* in Isa 45,9-13 by contrast might mirror the prophet's grief at the rebelliousness of the people[61]. But quite apart from the function of *hôy*, the lack of the clearly introduced quotation followed by a refutation in Amos 5,18-20; Isa 10,5-15; 29,15-16 and 45,9-13 is by itself sufficient reason to consider that these units do not belong with the texts which do display this structure.

A. S. van der Woude proposes three disputes in Micah, which he describes as examples of the genre *Disputationswort*[62]. In Mic 2,6-11, his first example, however, the words of the opposition in vv.6-7 are given rather as illustration of their reprehensible conduct than as the expression of an opinion to be refuted. Van der Woude distributes Mic 4,9-14 between the pseudo-prophets (vv.9.11-13) and Micah (vv.10.14) and describes the whole as *Disputationswort*. Even if his distribution of the verses is to be accepted, the material would have to be seen

---

[58] MELUGIN, *Isaiah 40-55*, 36-37, notes the similarities and describes Isa 10,15; 29,15-16 and 45,9-13 as "handler-handled" disputations.

[59] HARDMEIER, *Texttheorie*, 319.

[60] HARDMEIER, *Texttheorie*, 378.

[61] HARDMEIER, *Texttheorie*, 383.

[62] VAN DER WOUDE, "Micah in Dispute", 244-260. Van der Woude sets out to investigate the ideas supposedly held by the pseudo-prophets, and also to prove that the genre *Disputationswort* is well-attested in Micah. Thus pp. 246-247.

as a disputation in dialogue, rather than a disputation speech, in which the pro-phet reports an opposing view and then refutes it. Finally, van der Woude pro-poses that Mic 2,12 - 3,12 represents a discussion, the words of doom beginning in 3,1 being Micah's reply to the pseudo-prophets. This again should be describ-ed as a disputation, not as a disputation speech, provided the distribution of the verses is correct. In none of the examples can be found the disputation speech structure, with its intention of refuting a clearly reported view of the opposi-tion.

W. Zimmerli considers the disputation speech to be one of the characteristic forms found in Ezekiel[63]. In the disputation speech the prophet replies to words heard from those around him. The prophet's activity was not limited to the closed circle of his disciples. His words are also replies or challenges to statements of the people. Sometimes such quotations from the people simply illustrate their conduct, as in Ezek 8,12; 9,9 and 33,30. But on other occasions they begin the disputation speech in which the prophet replies to the quotation. Zimmerli lists the texts of Ezekiel where this process is found[64]. He also gives examples from other prophets, not all acceptable. In Isa 40,27-31 the process is clearly that of quotation followed by refutation as found in Ezekiel, in Jer 2,23 the quotation is refuted in one verse as part of a longer poem, but in Isa 30,16 the quotations are more illustrative of conduct, and in Isa 45,9-10 there is no formal expression of an opinion. Nevertheless, Zimmerli focuses attention on the disputation speech as the refutation of words heard by the prophet among his people[65].

The most precise description of the disputation speech as the formally in-troduced quotation of the people's words, which are then disputed by the pro-phet, the first of the forms indicated by Gunkel in his treatment of the disputa-tion, is given by C. Westermann almost by chance in a review[66]. He describes the basic structure of the disputation speech (*Streitgespräch*, *Disputationswort*, *Bestreitung*) as beginning with a statement or thesis which is contested with a counter-thesis. The development of the counter-thesis, and therefore the refuta-tion of the thesis, can take on various forms. It simply has to give reasons for the counter-thesis.

---

[63] ZIMMERLI, *Ezechiel*, 54*.

[64] ZIMMERLI, *Ezechiel*, 275, lists the disputation speeches in Ezekiel as 11,2ff; 11,15ff; 12,21-25; 12,26-28; 18,2ff; 20,32ff; 33,17ff; 33,24ff; 37,11-14. In place of 33,17ff, 33,10ff should be read, as is ap-parent from p. 798.

[65] EICHRODT, *Hesekiel*, 84, adopts a similar position though he reserves the term "disputation" for Malachi. HOSSFELD, *Untersuchungen*, 363-364, adopts Zimmerli's structure for the disputation speech, and also sees the speeches of Malachi as developments of the genre. He divides the disputation speeches in Ezekiel into two principal groups. Those with no command to the prophet to speak (Ezek 18; 20,32-38; 33,17-20) he describes as *Lehrrede*. FOHRER, *Ezechiel*, xx, considers there are six disputa-tion speeches *(Diskussionsworte)* in Ezekiel. They are 12,21-25; 12,26-28; 14,12-23; 15,1-8; 18,1-20 and 18,21-32. Fohrer gives no detailed justification for his list.

[66] WESTERMANN, Rezension BEUKEN, *Haggai*, 426.

Due to the lack of unanimity which characterises the question it is no surprise that introductions and general presentations of prophetic genres either
omit the disputation speech entirely or give incomplete accounts of it[67]. O.
Eissfeldt sees the disputation speech (*Streitgespräch*) in Deutero-Isaiah as a
suitable genre for asserting Yahweh's superiority over other gods[68]. Sellin and
Fohrer refer to the disputation speech as *Diskussionswort*[69]. Their brief summary of the processes involved in disputation speeches reflects the work of J.
Begrich. Fohrer later stresses that the disputation speech (again *Diskussionswort*) is a borrowed genre, not genuinely prophetic, which has the aim of
contradicting an objection[70]. J. Schreiner maintains that the disputation speech
contests an idea which is either stated or implied. This is done through questions and forms of proof which are not always strictly logical[71]. In the view of
A. Ohler, the disputation speech sets out to reply to objections and doubts of
the listeners[72]. Her principal example, Isa 28,23-29, however, does not make
such objections and doubts clear. The picture presented by W. E. March is
derived from the various contributions of C. Westermann[73]. K. Koch
acknowledges the existence of the disputation speech (*Streitgespräch*) in prophetic literature, but gives no idea of how he views its nature[74]. O. Kaiser finds
disputation speeches in Ezekiel, Deutero-Isaiah, Haggai and Malachi. In
Deutero-Isaiah he adopts the structure of basis (*Disputationsbasis*) and consequence (*Schlussfolgerung*)[75]. The recent contribution of W. H. Schmidt stresses
that it is through questions that the prophet tries to reach conclusions which
refute the listeners' doubts. The disputation speech reaches a stricter form in
Deutero-Isaiah and Malachi[76].

In all these introductory works various stages of the more detailed investigation are reflected. The chief problem facing all the studies of the disputation speech is the lack of a clear common structure. As R. R. Wilson states, in
the disputation speech "no structural patterns can be discerned"[77]. It is the aim
of this study to make clear the missing structural pattern, and investigate the
literary genre of which it is the basis.

---

[67] No mention is made of the disputation speech in their accounts of the genres of prophetic
literature by BENTZEN, *Introduction*; MUÑOZ IGLESIAS, *Los Géneros Literarios*; TUCKER, *Form Criticism of
the Old Testament*; TUCKER, "Form Criticism, OT"; RAMLOT, "Les moyens d'expression"; MONLOUBOU,
"Les Genres Prophétiques".

[68] EISSFELDT, *Einleitung*, 457.

[69] SELLIN, FOHRER, *Einleitung*, 390.

[70] FOHRER, *Das Alte Testament*, 28.

[71] SCHREINER, *Einführung*, 216.

[72] OHLER, *Gattungen*, Band 2, 50-52.

[73] MARCH, "Prophecy", 168.

[74] KOCH, *Formgeschichte*, 258, n. 1.

[75] KAISER, *Einleitung*, 240-241.

[76] SCHMIDT, *Einführung*, 188.

[77] WILSON, "Form-Critical Investigation", 108.

During this examination of how the disputation speech has been presented in genre study many texts sometimes given this designation have been considered unworthy of it. The reasons for their rejection as disputation speeches are now summarised.

1) In a great number of the texts proposed quotations of the people are given not in order to be refuted but as an illustration of the guilt of the people. The quotations in Isa 22,13b; 28,9-10 and 30,16 are examples. Such texts should not be regarded as disputation speeches.

2) In many texts proposed as disputation speeches the opinion of the people is implied and not explicitly stated. In such texts it can by no means always be presumed that the people did in fact think differently from the prophet. Furthermore, the structure is necessarily different from the disputation speeches with the quotation-refutation pattern. One text where it is strongly hinted that the people's opinion is being corrected is Amos 5,18-20, which might possibly be designated an "implicit disputation speech". However, the opening *hôy* in v.18 also has a bearing on the genre.

3) Texts belonging to other genres but which are considered as having an argumentative tone should not be called disputation speeches. Examples are the parables in Isa 5,1-7 and 28,23-29 and the trial speeches in Deutero-Isaiah. Argumentative tone is an insufficient criterion for genre designation.

4) A speech in which the argument proceeds from one point to another in a logical sequence of thought, but which betrays little or no trace of the opinion of the listeners, does not merit the designation disputation speech. A number of texts in Deutero-Isaiah frequently presented as disputation speeches fall into this category. Since there is no clear disagreement, the designation as disputation speeches is highly debatable.

5) The disputation speeches with the quotation-refutation pattern must be distinguished from those texts where a disputation is given in direct speech, where each of the parties speaks, as happens in Job. These latter texts are best described as "dialogue disputations". In the disputation speech only the prophet speaks, and reports the people's view himself.

6) The speeches of Malachi begin with an initial statement by God or by the prophet, which is followed after a question from the people by a full explanation. They are of a different genre from the disputation speech, which begins with a quotation of the people's words, which is then refuted. Their aim is to convince the listeners of the initial stated point, not to reject the listeners' quoted opinion.

7) Some speeches beginning with *hôy* sometimes referred to as disputation speeches do intend to challenge the opinions of others, but the introductory *hôy* considerably modifies the aim of the speeches by constituting a threat to the opponents. The genre designation "disputation speech" is therefore inadequate for speeches such as Isa 10,5-15.

8) A text may show the structure of quotation followed by refutation, and

the intention to refute the speaker's opinion, but not be an independent unit. An example is Jer 2,23a, which is part of the long poem which makes up Jer 2 and cannot be regarded as an autonomous disputation speech.

This drastic reduction of the number of speeches called disputation speeches has one aim: to give precision to the designation and make it readily comprehensible. The name "disputation speech" can worthily be given to those texts where an opinion of the speakers is explicitly reported by the prophet and refuted by him.

PART TWO

The Texts

The pattern of quotation followed by refutation lies at the basis of a clearly constructed literary genre which can justifiably be designated "disputation speech". From Isaiah to Haggai the prophets used this device to refute the people's false opinions. A close examination of the texts reveals how the literary genre developed.

Isaiah 28,14-19

Unity and Structure

The speech begins in v.14 with a call to listen to the word of Yahweh and a new addressee. V.23 will begin a further unit with a renewed call to attention. Vv.14-22, however, present two major problems regarding unity: the role of vv.16-17a is disputed, and it is questioned whether vv.19-22 belonged to the original speech.

Vv.16-17a have often been regarded as a promise and have been rejected as an addition because they do not fit in the supposed sequence of accusation followed by judgement[1]. Others have considered that Isaiah inserts these words of promise deliberately in the middle of a judgement speech, a phenomenon found elsewhere in Isaiah, as in 28,7-13, where v.12 provides the change of tone[2]. But it is by no means certain that vv.16-17a contain words of promise[3]. The structure of the disputation speech found here indicates that vv.16-17a in fact begin the refutation of the quotation found in v.15. They precede the explicit denial of that quotation which follows in vv.17b-18[4].

---

[1] Thus PROCKSCH, *Jesaia I*, 356-359; CHILDS, *Assyrian Crisis*, 28-31; KAISER, *Jesaja*, 201-203; VERMEYLEN, *Isaïe*, 392-395.

[2] WESTERMANN, *Grundformen*, 134, regards v.16 as offering a sign such as those given in salvation speeches. ALONSO SCHOEKEL, *Estudios*, 497, considers that vv.16-17a contain a brief announcement of restoration. MELUGIN, "The Conventional and the Creative", 306-309, stresses Isaiah's originality. BARTH, *Jesaja-Worte*, 11, considers that an announcement of disaster and of salvation are found in the same speech.

[3] WILDBERGER, *Jesaja*, 1076, maintains that vv.16-17a announce a coming test which will precede the judgement.

[4] DIETRICH, *Jesaja*, 166, has suggested that v.16 alone should be rejected, and thus stresses the contrasts between v.15b and v.17a. V.16, however, is necessary to understand v.17a. PETERSEN, "Isaiah 28", 111-112, extracts v.17b alone. This, however, would mean that the section of the quotation corresponding to v.17b would be the only section not explicitly denied.

The second major problem regarding the unity of the speech concerns vv.19-22, which have been rejected wholly or partially for various reasons[5]. The structure of the disputation speech finishes adequately but abruptly when v.18 is considered the close of the unit. The presence of ʿBR twice in v.19 suggests that this verse may well belong with what precedes, since ʿBR is prominent in the quotation (v.15). In vv.18b.19a a final crescendo is produced in the denial of the quotation by a triple use of ʿBR[6]. Vv.20.21, on the other hand, have no vocabulary links with the quotation, and introduce new motifs. The admonition in v.22 seems out of place, since judgement already appears inevitable. Further-more, vv.20-22 are more loosely connected with vv.14-19 by kî and wᵉʿattâ[7]. The resulting unit, vv.14-19, thus begins and ends with ŠMᶜ, which further strengthens the case for considering it the original speech.

Introduction

14   So, listen to the word of Yahweh,
        you men of arrogance,
        you who lay down the law
        for this people in Jerusalem.
15   For you have said:

The lākēn which begins the unit may well be an addition intended to weld the speech to what precedes[8]. It has little or no significance for the disputation speech, by contrast to lākēn in v.16, which, with the messenger formula, heralds the refutation. The call to attention which follows is found in no other disputa-tion speech. The call is addressed to "men of arrogance", those who rule in Jerusalem[9]. The expression "who lay down the law" is proposed here as an at-tempt to convey the double sense of MŠL, "to rule" and "to make proverbs", in an accepted idiomatic phrase[10]. MŠL will return in a reference to the making of proverbs in the disputation speech in Ezek 18,2-3; māšāl will appear both in Ezek 18,2-3 and 12,22.

---

[5] KAISER, Jesaja, 203-204, and VERMEYLEN, Isaïe, 389, consider all four verses secondary. WILDBERGER, Jesaja, 1070-1071, rejects vv.19.22 but considers vv.20-21 probably original.

[6] ALONSO SCHOEKEL, Estudios, 498. He considers vv.20-22 an appendix.

[7] MELUGIN, "The Conventional and the Creative", 309-310, suggests v.20 kî introduces a sapiential addition, and points out the different forms and images in vv.21-22.

[8] ALONSO SCHOEKEL, Estudios, 496; WILDBERGER, Jesaja, 1068. JONGELING, "Lākēn", 198, maintains that where lākēn is followed by an imperative the order given is always related to what precedes. Isa 28,14 would seem to be one case where this is not so.

[9] EXUM, "Isaiah 28-32", 137, has suggested that lāsôn, which lies parallel to bîrûšalaim, is an ironic pun on siyyôn.

[10] Contrast IRWIN, Isaiah 28-33, 25, who renders "reigning wits". WILDBERGER, Jesaja, 1064, 1072, is too categorical in his exclusion of the "reign" nuance.

The introduction makes clear that Isaiah is addressing a group who have some responsibility as leaders in Jerusalem, and addressing them in uncomplimentary fashion.

Quotation

15   We have made a treaty with Death,
       and with Sheol we have forged an agreement.
       The overflowing flood, when it passes,
       will not reach us.
       For we have made lies our shelter,
       and in deceit we have taken refuge.

          šôṭ and *ya'ăbōr* to be read with the Qere

This quotation is the longest in any disputation speech. The central statement of confidence, that the coming flood represents no danger, is preceded and followed by the reasons for such confidence, given both times in chiasm.

Since those speaking are called rulers, it is no surprise that their first boasts concern their prowess in forging treaties. *ḥōzeh*, which returns in v.18 as *ḥāzût*, is to be seen as related to *ḤZH* in the sense of "choose" found in Exod 18,21. It is thus to be rendered "agreement"[11]. The leaders boast that their treaties have been made with Death and Sheol. These phrases, unparalleled in the MT, express the unbounded confidence of the leaders in their political manoeuvres to win allies against Assyria[12]. Due to their political machinations they feel as safe as if they had actually made a treaty with the powers of death. They consider themselves to be immune from danger[13]. Their limitless arrogance leads them to boast not only of having no fear of death, but even of their astuteness in using lies and deceit as means for forging agreements. They boast of their unscrupulousness in their political dealings with Egypt[14]. The

---

[11] KUTSCH, *Verheissung*, 36-38, illustrates this sense of the root *ḤZH* not only from Exod 18,21, but also from Aramaic Dan 3,19 and texts from Palmyra. FUHS, *Sehen*, 316-317, follows Kutsch, considering Exod 18,21 alone sufficient proof for this sense of *ḤZH*.

[12] Wis 1,16 describes the "ungodly" *(asebeis)* as those who consider Death as a friend and make a covenant with it *(kai suntheken ethento pros auton)*. This verse begins a long description of the attitude of these men, who believe death to be the final end of man. Their attitude is rejected as erroneous in Wis 2,21-24. While in Isa 28,15 the words "treaty with Death" form part of a self-secure boast in the face of a particular danger, in Wis 1,16 they are part of the writer's description of the whole attitude to life of the ungodly.

[13] HUBER, *Jahwe, Juda und die anderen Völker*, 96, considers the quotation thus, but regards it as having been invented by Isaiah. KLOPFENSTEIN, *Die Lüge*, 148-149, suggests the quotation is the rulers' mocking reply to earlier words of Isaiah against them. There is in fact no compelling reason to deny the quotation to the leaders themselves, since it reflects their unbounded confidence and is quite true to life.

[14] WILDBERGER, *Jesaja*, 1073-1075, proposes that pagan rites seeking protection against the powers of death may lie behind the expressions concerning treaties with Death and Sheol. DUHM, *Jesaia*, 170,

powers of Death and Sheol are seen together again in Hezekiah's lament that Sheol cannot give thanks to Yahweh, nor Death praise him (Isa 38,18). Against these very powers the rulers feel secure. These words, however, also have an underlying theological connotation. Striving after political covenants to secure themselves from death implies scant regard for the true covenant with Yahweh himself.

The central statement of the quotation affirms boldly that the "overflowing flood" will not reach them. *šôṭ* should be read as in v.18. But the usual translation "scourge" does not fit with the verb *ŠṬP*[15]. It is necessary to understand *šôṭ* as "flood", a rendering not unknown in Hebrew tradition[16]. The rendering of *šôṭ* as "flood" is further advised by Isa 8,7-8, which speaks of the invasion of the Assyrians as the coming of the mighty waters of a great river. These waters will overflow (*ŠṬP*) and pass (*ʿBR*). The speakers in 28,15 state that the overflowing flood of an Assyrian invasion, when it passes, will not harm them. The onslaught of Assyria is again described as overflowing waters in Isa 28,2 and 30,28. This image will be developed in the refutation of the quotation in vv.17-19[17].

The two clauses closing the quotation show further reasons for confidence. The rulers have been astute in their political machinations, using lies and deceit as their instruments. They do not hesitate to boast of their unscrupulousness. But, as with *bᵉrît* in v.15, there is a deeper sense in the rulers' words. For just as Yahweh offers the only secure covenant, so also he is the true shelter and the secure refuge, as made abundantly clear in the Psalms[18]. By saying that they have chosen lies for their shelter and deceit for their refuge, they are implicitly rejecting Yahweh as the true refuge and shelter for his people.

The quotation thus is a true to life expression of the rulers' limitless arrogance. They voice their absolute confidence in the face of the Assyrian threat,

---

and SCHMIDT, *Die grossen Propheten*, 95, proposed that Death and Sheol represent Egyptian gods, possibly Osiris and Isis, for Israel sought protection from Egypt. It is quite possible that the speakers saw Death and Sheol as personified powers, perhaps even as gods, but the most apparent meaning of their words is that they literally feel secure against death due to their political arrangements.

[15] GESE, "Die strömende Geissel", 132, defends the rendering "scourge" and sees the expression as inspired by the image of Hadad, the weather god, with scourge in hand. He explains the attribute *šôṭēp* by appealing to *šôṭēp ṣᵉdāqâ* in Isa 10,22, where *ŠṬP* is used transitively. The parallel is inadequate, however, since *ŠṬP* has no object in 28,15 and thus must be intransitive, showing the rendering "scourge" to be unsuitable.

[16] BARTH, "שׁוֹט שֹׁטֵף", 306-307, indicated Arabic and Ethiopian parallels. POZNAŃSKI, "Zu שׁוֹט שֹׁטֵף", 119-120, gives examples of this sense from Targums and Hebrew tradition. WILDBERGER, *Jesaja*, 1065, also defends the translation "flood" due to the verbs *ŠṬP* and *ʿBR*, of which *šôṭ* is the subject.

[17] Extra-biblical uses of the image of storm and flood for an invading army are referred to by WILDBERGER, *Jesaja*, 326.

[18] God is described as *maḥseh* in Ps 14,6;46,2; 61,4; 62,8.9; 71,7; 73,28; 91,2.9; 94,22; 142,6. The verb *ḤSH* is used often of taking refuge in God, as GERSTENBERGER, "*ḥsh*", 622-623, illustrates. The root *STR* is used with reference to God's protection, e.g. in Ps 27,5; 31,21; 64,3, as WEHMEIER, "*str* hi.", 181, shows. *ḤSH* and *STR* reappear in Isa 4,6; 16,3.4 and 25,4.

for they are capable of forging treaties even with Death, and they rely fully on their cunning, using lies and deceit to come to political arrangements. They trust entirely in their own evil scheming and have rejected Yahweh as their suzerain and refuge.

Refutation

16   And so, thus says the Lord Yahweh:
        Look! I am founding on Sion a stone,
        a stone of testing, a corner-stone,
        precious as a foundation:
        the one who relies on it will not flee.
17   And I will make justice the measuring-line,
        and righteousness the level.
        And hail will sweep away the shelter of lies;
        as for the refuge, the waters will overwhelm it.
18   It will be annulled, your treaty with Death,
        and your agreement with Sheol will not stand.
        The overflowing flood will indeed pass,
        and you will be trampled by it.
19   As often as it passes, it will catch you.
        Morning by morning it will pass,
        by day and by night.
        And it will be sheer terror to understand
        the message.

> In v.17 *yissād* is to be read *yōsēd*, and *mûssād* is to be omitted as dittography.

As often happens in Ezekiel, *lākēn* and the messenger formula open the refutation[19]. Later on in the refutation, in vv.17b-18, each part of the quotation will be explicitly denied. But Yahweh begins by proposing an alternative to the leaders' dishonest striving after political arrangements. Yahweh takes up the motif of building shelters from the last part of the quotation, and announces that he himself will provide the foundations of a new refuge, on which men can rely. He announces the laying of a stone, and the applying of a measuring-line and level. These three actions symbolise Yahweh's alternative way to the rulers' dishonest political scheming. Thus he refutes their boastful assertions and their trust in the frail shelters of political agreements. Indeed, the first of the actions, the laying of the stone, is an invitation to trust in Yahweh.

The greatest emphasis is laid on this first act of Yahweh and in particular on the description of the stone. Yahweh announces that the stone will be laid in

---

[19] Thus also in Ezek 11,7.16.17; 12,23.28; 33,25 and 37,12.

the near future[20]. It is described as *'eben bōḥan*. This phrase is sometimes considered a technical designation for types of hard stone, and others see it as connected with the verb *BḤN*[21]. Since Yahweh's next actions in v.17a will involve
instruments of measurement, the measuring-line and the level, it seems more
probable that this stone too is used for some kind of test. The word *bōḥan*
would certainly suggest the idea of testing even if its original meaning were not
to be derived from *BḤN*[22]. The interpretation as "stone of testing" is made
more likely by the description of Yahweh in Isa 8,14 as a "stone of striking"
and a "rock of stumbling" for the two houses of Israel. Against the background
of the threat of invasion, the prophet is told that fear and awe should be reserved for Yahweh alone (8,13). In 28,16 too the real issue is that of fidelity to
Yahweh, not the question of political alliances in face of danger.

The "stone of testing" is to be established on Sion, the site of Yahweh's
presence and symbol of faith in him[23]. Sion is the site of the true refuge in contrast to the rulers' shelters of lies and deceit. In a similar vein, Isa 14,32 pro-
claims that Yahweh founded Sion and that the poor of his people would find
refuge *(ḤSH)* there. The stone is further described as "a corner-stone, precious
as a foundation"[24]. The corner-stone is the place where work on a building
begins. In Ps 118,22 Yahweh makes the stone rejected by the builders the
corner-stone of his building. The special stones needed for the foundation of the
temple and surrounding buildings are called *yᵉqārôt* in 1 Kgs 5,31 and 7,9-11.
And *mûsād* in 2 Chr 8,16 refers to the foundation of the house of Yahweh. Thus
each of the expressions describing the stone emphasises its importance and the

---

[20] *hinᵉnî yōsēd* is to be read. The only comparable uses to the MT's *hinᵉnî yissād*, Isa 29,14 and
38,5 (given in GKC 155f), are themselves dubious. The following *wᵉśamtî* indicates *yōsēd* should be
read. HUBER, *Jahwe, Juda und die anderen Völker*, 91, n.8, and PETERSEN, "Isaiah 28", 110, 121, n. 31,
take the participle obtained as a reference to the past, but there is no similar use of *hinnēh* and a participle as a reference to a once only action in the past. The texts from GKC 116 o which they call upon
for support (Gen 37,7; 41,17) use *hinnēh* and the participle to refer to repeated or continuous actions
in the past. But the same Gen 37,7 uses *hinnēh* and the qatal form *qāmâ* to refer to a once only action
in the past. Thus *yōsēd* here refers to the near future. IRWIN, *Isaiah 28-33*, 30-31, maintains the MT
vocalisation as the more difficult reading, but the parallels he cites, both Hebrew and Ugaritic, use
different forms. Ezek 25,7 *hinᵉnî nāṭîtî* seems rather to prove *hinᵉnî vissad* needs correction.
[21] TSEVAT, "*bḥn*", 591-592, suggests it is a stone used for the foundations of a fortress. WILDBERGER,
Jesaja, 1066-1067, rejects this and preserves the traditional connection with the verb "to test".
[22] WILDBERGER, *Jesaja*, 1076, sees the interpretation as "testing" as confirming his view that in v.16
the judgement is already being announced. EXUM, "Isaiah 28-32", 139, suggests a deliberate double
meaning in *bōḥan*.
[23] HUBER, *Jahwe, Juda und die anderen Völker*, 98; PORTEOUS, "Jerusalem-Zion", 240. *bᵉṣiyyôn* is
taken as an example of *bᵉ*-essentiae by HUBER, *Jahweh, Juda und die anderen Völker*, 91,n.9,98, and
IRWIN, *Isaiah 28-33*, 31. Such a rendering does not radically alter the sense.
[24] A parallel expression to *pinnat yiqrat mûsād* is found in Deut 21,11 *'ēšet yᵉpat-tō'ar*, as
WILDBERGER, *Jesaja*, 1067, notes. It therefore seems that *mûssād* should be considered dittography.
IRWIN, *Isaiah 28-33*, 31-32, maintains the consonantal text by taking *mûssād* as a hophal participle
mûssad and "nomen regens" to *hamma'ămîn*. He translates "founded by the Master Builder who hur-
ries not". But the use of *'MN* in Isa 7,9 militates against this interpretation.

firmness of its foundation. The gradual accumulation of words reflects the gradual building up of Yahweh's building[25].

It is then explicitly stated what this "stone of testing" symbolises. The final phrase "the one who relies on it will not flee" makes clear that it is a symbol of trust in Yahweh. The verb *ḤWŠ* can be interpreted "hasten" or "flee", an intransitive use like that in Isa 5,19, where the subject is the deed of Yahweh, the quick execution of which is awaited[26]. The weight of the phrase, however, lies on the word *hamma'ămîn*. The one who will have no need to flee is the one who finds his support in the stone Yahweh lays, the one who trusts in Yahweh. The firm building Yahweh constructs is worthy of trust, unlike the petty shelters the rulers have erected. A similar situation lies behind Isa 7,9, where the prophet says to Ahaz: "if you do not trust *(ta'ămînû)*, you will not be supported *(tē'āmēnû)*". Ahaz is bidden to trust Yahweh rather than seek a political alliance with Assyria against Aram and Ephraim. Similarly, in 28,16, trust in Yahweh is to be preferred to striving after political alliances[27].

The stone which Yahweh lays is then a symbol of trust in him. It is a challenge to the rulers' confidence in political scheming. It presents a test in which the rulers will be found wanting. But Yahweh in v.17a will apply two further tests with the measuring-line of justice and the level of righteousness, tests similar to those applied in Isa 5,7. *wᵉśamtî* here contrasts with the leaders' *śamnû* in v.15. The measuring-line and the level are found in the same metaphorical sense in 2 Kgs 21,13 as yardsticks of judgement for Jerusalem, while in Isa 34,11 Yahweh judges with the "measuring-line of chaos".

In vv.16-17a the prophet thus challenges the leaders' confidence and conduct and shows through the symbol of the new building that Yahweh's way to salvation is not through political and military alliances and scheming, but through justice and righteousness built on the foundation of reliance on Yahweh. These words represent a test for the leaders, a test they have clearly failed. They knew Yahweh's way was that of trust in him, but they put their trust in political scheming. They knew Yahweh's building was constructed with justice and righteousness, but they preferred to build shelters of lies and deceit. Vv.17b-19 now make explicit the rejection of the rulers' claims by denying each section of the quotation, culminating in an extended denial of the central statement of confidence that the waters of the Assyrian advance represent no danger.

The refutation in vv.16-17a took up the theme of building, and so the first part of the quotation to be explicitly renounced is the leaders' boasting of their

---

[25] Thus EXUM, "Isaiah 28-32", 139.

[26] WILDBERGER, *Jesaja*, 1067-1068, considers the variety of renderings in the LXX, Vg and Syriac versions and in the NT citations (1 Pet 2,6; Rom 9,33; 10,11), and the consequent suggestions to emend the text. He concludes that the meaning "flee" is the correct one.

[27] JEPSEN, "*'aman*", 330, stresses the similarity between the two texts. WILDBERGER, *Jesaja*, 1077 considers that, like 7,9, Isa 28,16 is by its sense a conditional sentence.

shelters of lies and deceit. The destruction of these shelters is at hand. Then it is announced that even pacts with Death and Sheol are of no avail[28]. Finally, the rulers' statement of supreme confidence that the overflowing flood will not catch them, that Assyria is no threat to them, is roundly denied. They will be trampled underfoot, a threat found too in Isa 5,5 and 10,6. This climax is prolonged into v.19 as repeated Assyrian onslaughts are foreseen. V.19b finally imagines the terror of those who understand this message of coming disaster, a terror made more exquisite by realising too late that an alternative and better way was always open, the way of trust in Yahweh[29].

Conclusion

The refutation of the quotation in this disputation speech performs several tasks. Not only does it deny the quotation explicitly in vv.17b-19, but also, in vv.16-17a, offers an alternative way. Vv.16-17a are essential to the unit, which would otherwise be reduced practically to a simple negation of the quotation. Vv.16-17a represent a challenge: to the leaders they are a judgement, for they have not trusted Yahweh nor practised justice and righteousness; for those who trust Yahweh, however, they contain a promise of safety. Analysis of the unit as a disputation speech thus allows both the elements of judgement and of promise to be seen in their true light. But the basic point of the unit is, as in Isa 7,9, the rejection of trust in political scheming. The true way to safety is that of trust in Yahweh. His is the true covenant, his building is the true shelter.

Jeremiah 8,8-9

Unity and Context

Jer 8,8-9 displays the disputation speech structure within two verses. The introduction in v.8a addresses the people in the second person plural, but v.9 returns to the third person address found in vv.4-7. The quotation in v.8a might well be understood as giving the people's indignant reaction to the prophet's words in vv.4-7. The prophet maintains that the people are unwilling to return to Yahweh; the verb ŠWB is prominent in vv.4-6. V.7 then contrasts the birds, which instinctively know times and seasons, with the people of Yahweh, who have no knowledge of his precepts. It could well be this reproach of ignorance

---

[28] ḥāzût is to be rendered "agreement" as ḥōzeh in v.15. Thus Kutsch, Verheissung, 36-38; Fuhs, Sehen, 316-317.

[29] Melugin, "The Conventional and the Creative", 309, and Exum, "Isaiah 28-32", 140, stress the link between v.19b and vv.16-17a: the message is all the more terrible because the way-out was not accepted.

of Yahweh's will which provokes the people's proud words in v.8. The disputation speech in vv.8-9 thus has links with vv.4-7[30].

Vv.10-12, which are omitted in the LXX, are largely a repetition of Jer 6,12-15. In Jer 6 the material is more securely attached to the context, since Jer 6,11 has already begun the detailed announcement of punishment. In Jer 8 vv.10-12 are a secondary addition, added perhaps to make v.9a more explicit[31]. It has also been proposed that v.13 belongs with 8,8-9. The verse would indicate how the wisdom of the Law produces nothing and provide a reply to the rhetorical question in v.9b[32]. But the figurative language in v.13 goes better with what follows. It begins a new section, where the description of the coming disaster is much more explicit and colourful[33]. The rhetorical question in v.9b thus brings this short disputation speech to an end. Vv.4-7 and vv.8-9 are two related units, to which vv.10-12 have been added.

Introduction and Quotation

8   How can you say:
       We are wise,
       for we possess the Law of Yahweh?

The combination of '*êk* and '*MR* to form a question is found often, but only here does it have the function of introducing an independent unit containing a quotation which is then formally refuted. '*êk* '*MR* is used to challenge the words of another in direct speech in Gen 26,9; Judg 16,15 and Ps 11,1. In 2 Sam 12,18 the same introduction asks how a piece of unwelcome news is to be communicated. In three prophetic texts '*êk* '*MR* introduces a quotation within a larger poem. In Jer 2,23a the indignant question "How can you say: I am not defiled. I have not gone after the Baals?" receives a reply with the words "Look at your footprints in the valley, admit what you have done!" Thus a complete, though not autonomous, disputation speech is found in one half-verse[34]. Similar questions in Jer 48,14 "How can you say: We are warriors, men-at-arms ready for war?" and in Isa 19,11 "How can you say to Pharaoh: I am a disciple of wise men, a disciple of ancient kings?" have no formal refutation, and are more akin

---

[30] KLOPFENSTEIN, *Die Lüge*, 133, stresses the connection between the people's words in v.8 and vv.4-7. So also BRIGHT, *Jeremiah*, 64; LUNDBOM, *Jeremiah*, 53-55. RUDOLPH, *Jeremia*, 61, however, sees vv.8-9 as addressed to "the wise" and having no relation with vv.4-7, its placing being due to the link between *mišpāṭ* in v.7 and *tôrâ* in v.8.

[31] WEISER, *Jeremia*, 72-73.

[32] Thus DUHM, *Jeremia*, 90; HYATT, "Torah", 382; WEISER, *Jeremia*, 73; HOLLADAY, *Jeremiah 1-20*, 99.

[33] ALONSO SCHOEKEL, SICRE DÍAZ, *Profetas*, I, 461-462, propose that Jer 8,13 begins a dialogue section between God, the people and the prophet, which ends in 9,2. God's threat in 8,13 begins this dialogue.

[34] In the same poem Jer 3,1 is a "self-condemnation parable" with a similar structure to Isa 5,1-7. Thus GRAFFY, "Isaiah 5,1-7", 408.

to the narrative uses of *'êk 'MR* where no reply is given, since no reply is necessary. Jeremiah's use of this introduction here stresses his indignation at the people's conceit.

The quotation itself is, like Isa 19,11, a boast of wisdom. The connection between wisdom and the possession of the Law is found only here in Jeremiah. In 4,22 the people are derided as "wise for doing wrong". But an arrogance similar to that expressed in 8,8 is found in 18,18: even while plotting against Jeremiah they still appear to revere the Law of the priests, as also the counsel of the sages and the word of the prophets. In fact, the overwhelming majority of references to the Law in Jeremiah explicitly refer to the people's lack of regard for it. It is the Law, which they do not in fact obey, which they now make the basis of their claim to wisdom and their defence against the prophet who has accused them of not knowing the precepts of Yahweh[35].

Refutation

8   But look! the lying pen of the scribes
        has made it into a lie!
9   The wise will be put to shame,
        they will be shattered and trapped.
        Look! they have rejected the word of Yahweh!
        So what use will their wisdom be to them?

> A mappiq must be added to *ᶜšh*.
> For *ḥkmt* read *ḥkmtm* (haplography).

'ākēn here begins the refutation, and is thus better given a contrasting force rather than its more common positive tone. The contrast is heightened by *hinnēh*. In spite of the frequency of *šeqer* in Jeremiah, the phrase *laššeqer ᶜŚH* is found only here, though similar phrases *ŠBᶜ laššeqer* (5,2; 7,9) and *NB' laššeqer* (27,15) are also used by Jeremiah. *šeqer* is often used in the context of false prophecy and with reference to idols, and basically means that which is false and therefore ineffective[36].

The scribes are only mentioned as a group here in Jeremiah. Jer 2,8, however, refers to the "experts in the Law" and declares that they do not know Yahweh. These "experts" must be a similar group to the scribes of 8,8, who

---

[35] The uses of *tôrâ* in Jeremiah have a generally negative tone. The context is usually one of rejection of the Law (6,9; 9,12; 16,11; 26,4; 32,23; 44,10.23) or of arrogance in possession of the Law (2,8; 8,8; 18,18). The only positive use is found in the new covenant text, 31,33.

[36] OVERHOLT, *The Threat*, 92, sums up the things which are called *šeqer* in Jeremiah as "the misconception of the nature of the security afforded by Yahweh's election of the nation, the words of his prophetic opponents, confidence in other gods". Something described as *šeqer* is ineffective, powerless to change the situation. The Law of Yahweh has been rendered powerless and ineffectual by the activity of the scribes.

were not merely copiers of the Law but also interpreted it[37]. Jer 18,18 suggests
that the priests were to some degree at least responsible for the Law, and that
these scribes were indeed a priestly group[38]. It is they, the priestly scribes, who
have tampered with the Law[39].

Quite apart from the question of who was falsifying the Law, it is not apparent what Law was being falsified. The Law referred to here might be
Deuteronomy, at least in the form that it had at that time[40]. Thus vv.8-9 would
amount to a condemnation of the deuteronomic reform and of the scribes who
fraudulently imposed it[41]. The text, however, does not refer explicitly to any
code of Law, and cannot be taken as showing Jeremiah's opposition to the
reform. It seems a general reference to Law, though one might suppose that the
new code of Deuteronomy would have been uppermost in Jeremiah's mind[42]. It
has been suggested by reference to Jer 7,21-22 that what is being condemned
here is an inordinate concentration on cultic legislation[43]. It is ill-advised to
limit the meaning of the text only to this sphere of legislation. The exact nature
of the perversion of the Law wrought by the scribes is not explained.

Attention is focused once again in v.9 on the people, those who consider
themselves wise, trusting exclusively in the written Law. General terms of
punishment announce their downfall in v.9a. The terms used here are often
employed to announce punishment, as in the oracles against Moab (48,1.20.39)
and against Babylon (50,2; 51,56). In Jeremiah the second hiphil form of BWŠ
which is found here has a sense similar to the qal, with the nuance that shame
is brought upon a person through his own fault[44]. The qatal and wayyiqtol
forms are to be taken as prophetic, and thus referring to the future.

A further reason is then given for the people's downfall, which makes their
attitude to the prophet quite clear: "they have rejected the word of Yahweh".
While apparently being devoted to the Law, they have turned a deaf ear to the
living word proclaimed by the prophet. In Jer 6,19 the people were accused of

---

[37] HYATT, "Torah", 384-387.

[38] OVERHOLT, *The Threat*, 82, considers the scribes mentioned here to have been government of-
ficials, since the scribal office before the exile was a secular one. It seems, however, from Jer 18,18
that the priests were already well involved with the Law. The same conclusion is indicated by Mic
3,11; Ezek 7,26 and by EICHRODT, *Theologie*, I, 45. OVERHOLT refers to BLACK, "Scribe", 246, where it is
stated that the term *sōpēr* never appears to have been applied to the priestly guardians of the Law
before the exile. The use of the term in Jer 8,8 appears to apply to just such a group. KUEHLEWEIN,
"*sēfaer*", 167, sees the use of the term in Jer 8,8 as the first time that the word is referred to an expert
in the Law, rather than simply to a scribe.

[39] CARROLL, *From Chaos*, 160-161, states that it is the "wise men" who are condemned here because
they have falsified the Law. In fact, no such group is mentioned here. Those under attack are the
scribes, for falsifying the Law, and the people, who consider themselves wise because they possess the
Law.

[40] Thus DUHM, *Jeremia*, 88.

[41] Thus also, for example, SCHMIDT, *Die grossen Propheten*, 249-250, who considers *tôrâ* here to
refer exclusively to Deuteronomy, and suggests Jeremiah had discovered it to be a fraud.

[42] Thus HYATT, "Torah", 383-384; RUDOLPH, *Jeremia*, 62-63; WEISER, *Jeremia*, 72.

[43] RUDOLPH, *Jeremia*, 61-62; WEISER, *Jeremia*, 72.

[44] SEEBASS, "*bôš*", 579-580; STOLZ, "*bōš*", 271.

not listening to Yahweh's words and of rejecting the Law. Here their apparent reverence for the Law is condemned, for it has not allowed them to see the perversions wrought in the Law by the scribes, and above all because it has led them to reject the word preached by the prophet.

The refutation concludes with the rhetorical question "what use will their wisdom be to them?" No reply is needed, though a redactor has added vv.10-12 to ensure the message is understood.

Conclusion

This disputation speech challenges the people's arrogant assertion that by mere possession of the Law they possess true wisdom. This wisdom of theirs has deceived them. They have been unable to recognise the perversions of the Law, for they have rejected Yahweh's word.

Jeremiah 31,29-30

Unity and Context

Jer 31,29-30 lies between two other units, vv.27-28 and vv.31-34, both introduced by "behold, the days are coming". The delimitation of the disputation speech is therefore clear, as is its simple structure.

The Text

29   In those days they will no longer say:
        The fathers ate sour grapes,
        but the sons' teeth are set on edge.
30   But they will say:
        Each one dies for his own sin.
        Every man who eats sour grapes
        will have his teeth set on edge.

Both the formula "in those days" and "behold, the days are coming" introduce future changes for the better in Jeremiah[45]. In this text, however, the nature of the future change is not immediately apparent. A reading of the Hebrew text without due consideration of the force of *kî 'im* produces the impression that the people will no longer repeat their proverb, but that each one

---

[45] JENNI, "*jōm*", 720-721.

will die for his own sin. In fact, the statement is well-balanced, and the meaning is apparent when it is realised that not only *lō' 'MR ᶜôd* but also *kî 'im* introduces words of the people. In those future days the people will no longer say one thing, but they will say another.

Other occurrences of the pattern *lō' 'MR ᶜôd ... kî 'im ...* in Jeremiah, preceded by one or other of the formulae concerning future days, show this to be the correct interpretation[46]. Jer 16,14-15 (parallel 23,7-8) announces that in future days an oath referring to the exodus from Egypt will be replaced by another concerning the liberation from the land of the north and other places of dispersal. The pattern is found here exactly as in Jer 31,29-30, but it is not an opinion which is being disputed. One saying simply replaces another. Jer 7,32 (parallel 19,6 with *QR'*) uses the same pattern to announce that the Valley of Tophet or Ben-hinnom will have its name changed to "valley of slaughter". In each of these cases the words "they will say" are to be understood after *kî 'im*. Jer 3,16-17 uses a similar pattern but omits *kî 'im* and does not directly replace one phrase by another. The pattern is found without explicit reference to future days to announce a change of name in Gen 17,5 (Abram to Abraham); 17,15 (Sarai to Sarah); 32,29; 35,10 (Jacob to Israel); Isa 62,4 (Sion's new names). The omission of *kî* in Gen 17,5 and *ôd* in Gen 17,15 does not change the basic sense. Finally, a free reverse formulation omitting *kî 'im* announces a future change of name in Hos 2,18.

Thus the pattern *lō' 'MR (QR') ᶜôd ... kî ('im) ...* is used predominantly to announce a change of name or saying. But there is one other instance where, as in Jer 31,29-30, the pattern is employed to challenge a mistaken opinion. Ezek 12,23 gives as part of the refutation of the quotation in v.22 a new quotation to be substituted for the old. V.23 uses the pattern *lō' MŠL 'ōtô ᶜôd ... kî 'im ...* Whereas, in Ezek 12,23, the pattern is found as part of the refutation in the disputation speech Ezek 12,21-25, in Jer 31,29-30 it provides the framework for the complete disputation speech.

The variations on the basic pattern can be listed thus:

Jer 31,29-30	*lō' 'MR ᶜôd*	*kî 'im*
Jer 16,14-15	*lō' 'MR ᶜôd*	*kî 'im*
Jer 23,7-8	*lō' 'MR ᶜôd*	*kî 'im*
Jer 7,32	*lō' 'MR ᶜôd*	*kî 'im*
Jer 19,6	*lō' QR' ᶜôd*	*kî 'im*
Jer 3,16-17	*lō' 'MR ᶜôd*	*bāᶜēt hahî'*
Gen 17,5	*lō' QR''ôd*	*wᵉhāyâ*
Gen 17,15	*lō' QR'*	*kî*
Gen 32,29	*lō' 'MR ᶜôd*	*kî 'im*

---

[46] SCHARBERT, *Solidarität*, 219-220; SCHONEVELD, "Jeremia xxxi,29,30", 341, and BOEHMER, *Heimkehr*, 130, n. 83, list other texts using the same pattern.

Gen 35,10	lōʾ QRʾ ʿôd	kî ʾim
Isa 62,4	lōʾ ʾMR ʿôd (X2)	kî
Ezek 12,23	lōʾ MŠL ʿôd	kî ʾim
(Hos 2,18	QRʾ	lōʾ QRʾ ʿôd)

The quotation in Jer 31,29 is similar to that found in Ezek 18,2, but with some minor differences. Ezekiel uses the yiqtol of ʾKL in place of Jeremiah's qatal, giving the quotation a general sense, and adds the definite article to bānîm. The presence of the same quotation in these two prophets and of similar words in Lam 5,7 indicates that such complaints concerning God's justice were widespread. The people considered they were being punished unjustly for the sins of their fathers.

The refutation looks forward to the time when they will speak differently. The change which is announced in this text is a change in knowledge of Yahweh's ways. In the future time of salvation they will no longer put all the blame for the events of 587 on their ancestors, but will recognise that they too had a share in the guilt[47].

The discovery of the pattern and its use in a disputation speech, in which an opinion of the people is being corrected, shows that the usual translations and consequent interpretations of the text fall far short of a true rendering[48]. A word-for-word translation (without the words "but they will say") leaves the impression that in the future the people will no longer repeat their proverb about collective punishment because God will begin to punish individually. This is naturally often interpreted as implying that until that future point God has punished and will continue to punish collectively[49]. In fact, since what is announced is a coming growth in understanding by the people, the implication is that God never in fact punished collectively. Jer 31,29-30 is not concerned with God's ways of punishment as the primary issue. It concerns the people's future awareness that it is God's way to judge individually, and therefore justly. That what is at issue is in fact a change of opinion, a change of heart, is made even more evident by the following unit, vv.31-34, which announces the new covenant. In the future, when God's law will be written on the hearts of men, they will have a deeper understanding of his ways[50].

---

[47] Thus, most clearly, BOEHMER, Heimkehr, 73.

[48] RSV: "In those days they shall no longer say: 'The fathers have eaten sour grapes, and the children's teeth are set on edge.' But every one shall die for his own sin; each man who eats sour grapes, his teeth shall be set on edge." TOB: "En ce temps-là, on ne dira plus: 'Les pères ont mangé du raisin vert et ce sont les enfants qui en ont les dents rongées!' Mais non! Chacun mourra pour son propre péché, et si quelqu'un mange du raisin vert, ses propres dents en seront rongées."

[49] GIESEBRECHT, Jeremia, 171; VOLZ, Jeremia, 279; RUDOLPH, Jeremia, 200; WEISER, Jeremia, 285; CARROLL, From Chaos, 214.

[50] RUDOLPH, Jeremia, 200-201, presented the difficulty that it is impossible to reconcile Yahweh's forgiveness in v.34 with the death of each sinner in v.30. This difficulty disappears with the interpretation of vv.29-30 given here for Yahweh can clearly announce forgiveness to a people which realises how just his ways are.

The objection might be raised that it is only v.30b which gives new words for the people to replace their former proverb, and that consequently the words "each one dies for his own sin" in v.30a do not form part of their future words. This view gains support from the similarity of the old proverb to v.30b alone. But *kî 'im* in the other texts considered is always followed either immediately by the new saying or name or by the verbs *QR'* or *DBR* (as in Ezek 12,23). The first words, "each one dies for his own sin", are therefore best seen as the first part of the words of the people, a prior explanation of the meaning of the new quotation. V.30a in fact makes the whole point of the disputation speech clear, and leaves no doubt about the exact meaning of the initial proverb.

Conclusion

This disputation speech challenges the idea of collective punishment. Jeremiah's challenge is, however, indirect. Ezek 18 will be more forthright in its rejection of collective retribution. Whereas Jeremiah speaks of a future change in the people's understanding of God's ways, Ezek 18,4 states categorically that it is the person who sins who dies. But both texts represent a challenge to those passages of the Law which state that Yahweh punishes the sins of the fathers to the third and fourth generation, Exod 34,7 and Num 14,18. These texts do not have the mitigating words "of those who hate me" found in the Decalogue, Exod 20,5 and Deut 5,9. Jeremiah and Ezekiel in fact make the same point as Deut 7,10; 24,16 and 2 Kgs 14,6, which defend individual retribution[51].

Jer 31,29-30 thus proposes the idea of individual retribution, but in the context of a disputation speech, and thus to announce that the present opinion of the people is mistaken. By announcing the coming change in their understanding of the ways of God the prophet at the same time refutes their present position.

Jeremiah 33,23-26

Context and Structure

This is the final unit of Jer 30-33, and is introduced by the formula of the

---

[51] It is significant that Jer 32,18a seems to uphold collective punishment by describing God as the one who "exacts punishment for the sins of the fathers from their sons after them". This statement is softened in v.19b which says that God "gives to each one according to his ways and the fruit of his acts". The same latter statement is found in Jer 17,10. In Jer 32,18a the prophet seems to have used a fixed formula, similar to Exod 34,7, to refer to God's kindness and his retribution, and to have been unmindful of the contradiction created with v.19b, and with 31,29-30. Thus SCHARBERT, *Solidarität*, 217, n. 347.

coming of the word. The delimitation of the unit thus presents no problem. In content and in expression the unit is similar to the preceding unit, vv.19-22, and also to 31,35-37. All deal with the lasting nature of Yahweh's covenant, and all use the solemn conditional *'im ... gam ...* But only 33,23-26 has the disputation speech structure: the solemn oath is used to refute the quotation. In the other two units the solemn conditional is simply introduced by the messenger formula (twice in 31,35-37 and once in 33,19-22).

This disputation speech presents one minor variation on the normal structure, the insertion of an explanatory remark of Yahweh between the quotation and the refutation in v.24b.

Introduction

23   The word of Yahweh came to Jeremiah, saying:
24   Have you not noticed what this people has said:

As frequently happens in the disputation speeches of Ezekiel, the formula of the coming of the word introduces the speech. Yahweh addresses a question to the prophet regarding the people's words, as in Ezek 12,22 and 18,2. *R'H* is used with the sense of perceiving[52]. "This people" is exclusively Israel/Judah in Jeremiah and very often has a pejorative tone, as in 8,5; 13,10 and 19,11. But in this case the presence of *ʿammî* as an object in the explanatory remark in v.24b is somewhat perplexing[53]. The text is to be explained by considering "this people" as limited to those among the Jews who thought of themselves as no longer being God's chosen people[54]. Certain elements among the people are quick to conclude from the turn of events that Yahweh has abandoned his people. They seem glad to be finally free of the onus of being a special people, bound to Yahweh by covenant. It is these individuals, "this people" (v.24a), who despise "my people" (v.24b) as having lost Yahweh's favour.

Quotation.

24   The two clans which Yahweh chose
        he has rejected?

mišpāḥâ in Jeremiah usually refers to the tribes of Israel or to the

---

[52] Thus also in Jer 3,6; 7,17. VETTER, "*r'h*", 693-694.

[53] For this reason DUHM, *Jeremia*, 276, and CORNILL, *Jeremia*, 373, suggested changes in the text of v.24b to refer the main verb to Yahweh: thus they read *ʿammô yin'aṣ* and *lepānāyw*. GIESEBRECHT, *Jeremia*, 186-187, on the other hand, proposed to change *lipnêhem* to *lepānāy*.

[54] VOLZ, *Jeremia*, 311.

nations[55]. The reference here to "two clans" is unique. It has sometimes been seen as designating David and Levi, mentioned in the previous unit[56]. But the lack of reference to Levi in the refutation tells against this. In the context of Yahweh's choice and covenant the reference is more probably to Israel and Judah, the two clans who in their ideal united state had become Yahweh's people. Jer 8,3 uses *mišpāḥâ* to refer to Judah, and further support for this interpretation might be gleaned from Ezek 35,10, where *šᵉnê haggôyim* and *šᵉttê hā'ărāṣôt* refer to Israel and Judah. *M'S* is found in Jeremiah predominantly of Yahweh's rejection of his people, notably in the coming refutation (v.26) and in the parallel in 31,37.

Explanatory Remark

24   And they despise my people
        as no longer being a nation in their eyes.

This section presents a comment by Yahweh on the quotation, a minor variation in the disputation speech structure. A similar extra remark is seen in Ezek 11,4-6. Yahweh's comment illustrates the quotation. Not only do the speakers consider that Yahweh has rejected his people, but they also believe that Israel and Judah can no longer be considered a nation[57]. But Yahweh already gives an idea of his coming reply by calling the "two clans" "my people".

Refutation

25   Thus says Yahweh:
        If I had not made my covenant
        with day and night,
        if I had not laid down rules
        for heaven and earth,
26   then would I reject the descendants
        of Jacob and of David my servant,

---

[55] Jer 2,4; 3,14; 31,1 use *mišpāḥâ* of Israel. Jer 1,15; 10,25; 25,9 of foreigners.

[56] Thus DUHM, *Jeremia*, 276; VOLZ, *Jeremia*, 311. Contrast CORNILL, *Jeremia*, 374; GIESEBRECHT, *Jeremia*, 187; RUDOLPH, *Jeremia*, 219; WEISER, *Jeremia*, 307, who see the "two tribes" as the two kingdoms.

[57] *gôy* in contrast to *ᶜam* refers to the people as a nation among the nations, and thus capable of international relations. Thus CODY, "Chosen People", 5; HULST, "ᶜam/gōj", 315-318. Similar contempt is expressed in Sir 50,25, where the inhabitants of Shechem are described as "not being a people" (ᶜm; LXX *ethnos*).

and would not take from his seed
rulers for the heirs of Abraham,
Isaac and Jacob!
For I will restore their fortunes
and have compassion on them.

> *yômām* to be read *yôm* (dittography).
> *'āšîb* to be read with the Qere (cf. 33,7.11).

The messenger formula, found so often at the beginning of the refutation in Ezekiel's more formal style, now introduces the formal reply. The refutation consists of a solemn oath with the conditional *'im ... gam ...*, a pattern found four times in Jeremiah, exclusively in this passage and its parallels, 31,36.37 and 33,20-21. The protasis refers to Yahweh's covenant with day and night (parallel to 33,20), and his rules for heaven and earth (parallel to 31,36): thus, the impossible condition is laid down that Yahweh does not in fact have absolute control over all time and all space[58].

The apodosis brings together the descendants of Jacob and of David, combining the "descendants of Israel" of 31,36.37 with the "descendants of David my servant" of 33,22. This final unit thus stresses Yahweh's fulfilment of his promises both to the Patriarchs and to David. The assurance is made more specific with the promise of rulers from his (David's) seed. This promise of *mōšᵉlîm* contrasts with the more specific promise of a *mōlēk* in 33,21, which is followed by an assurance to the Levites. Yahweh's continuing commitment to his people is expressed in more general terms in the concluding clause. The restoring of fortunes is a major theme of Jer 30-33, and the phrase is found again in a similar concluding clause preceded by *kî* in 32,44 and 33,11.

Conclusion

The three similar units, 31,35-37; 33,19-22 and 33,23-26, all affirm the lasting nature of Yahweh's covenant with Israel and David. But 33,23-26 gives an indication of the concrete situation which gave rise to such repeated solemn promises. The words in the quotation in v.24 set down the feelings of some members of God's people that he has finally rejected Israel and Judah. To these doubting words Yahweh's reply affirms solemnly that he will stand by his people and restore their fortunes.

---

[58] *bᵉrîtî* must be maintained due to the parallel in 33,20. The double *lō'* is emphatic. *bārā'tî* is suggested as the correct reading by DUHM, *Jeremia*, 277, and CORNILL, *Jeremia*, 373. *BR'* is in fact only found once in Jeremiah, in 31,22. Indeed there is no place in MT where *BR'* has as its object *yôm* and *lāylâ*, though references to the creation of light and darkness (Gen 1,3-5; Isa 45,7) may amount to the same thing. Quite apart from all this, the text makes perfect sense as it stands.

Ezekiel 11,2-12

Context and Structure

The major vision which lies in Ezek 8-11, and is finally brought to a close in 11,22-25, has been added to in a variety of ways[59]. The material introduced in 11,1-13.14-21 concerns a quite different issue. Whereas the major vision in Ezek 8-11 deals with cultic transgressions and their punishment, the destruction of the inhabitants of the city, 11,1-13.14-21 are concerned rather with the political questions of the status of the new rulers of Jerusalem and the fate of the exiles. Furthermore, Ezek 11,1-13 presents a new and different vision inserted within the major vision of Ezek 8-11. Ezek 11,1 announces a new transportation of the prophet, like that narrated in 8,3, but now to the east gate of the temple. He finds himself in the presence of a group of twenty-five men. This minor vision is quite separate from what precedes, for Ezek 9 had already narrated God's judgement on all evil men in the city. V.1 in fact provides the setting for a speech of the prophet in vv,2-12 which is a disputation speech. The minor vision is concluded in v.13 with the account of the dramatic effect of Ezekiel's words, the sudden death of Pelatiah. The name of Pelatiah occurs in both v.1 and v.13, the two verses of the vision framework, and k^ehinnābe'î in v.13 refers back to Ezekiel's disputation speech in vv.2-12. Thus the disputation speech in vv.2-12 is set in a vision which has been inserted in the major vision of Ezek 8-11.

The disputation speech displays two not unparalleled variations on the basic structure. Additional words from Yahweh come between quotation and refutation in vv.4-6. A similar additional remark of Yahweh is found in Jer 33,24b. The disputation speech also contains a double refutation, a device used also in Ezek 11,14-17;33,23-29; Isa 49,14-25 and Hag 1,2.4-11.

Introduction

2   And he said to me:
           Son of man, these are the men
           who contrive iniquity,
           who plan plans of evil in this city.
3   These are the men who say:

The formula of the coming of the word, which often introduces Ezekiel's disputation speeches, is absent due to the insertion of the speech in the minor vision. The men Ezekiel sees are said to be contriving iniquity. Mic 2,1 also uses the phrase ḤŠB 'āwen, and again with a parallel rā^c, in a similar context of usur-

---

[59] ZIMMERLI, *Ezechiel*, 202.

pation of property. The parallel participle of 'MR serves as the immediate introduction to the quotation.

Quotation

3   We have plenty of time to build up the houses;
       (literally: Houses will not be built up soon)
       this is the pot, and we are the meat.

The first part of the quotation allows a wide variety of interpretations both due to its apparent ambiguity, and due to the fact that it is not explicitly refuted. The infinitive construct might be construed as a statement, a question, or even a command. *b^enôt bāttîm* can obviously refer to the actual construction of houses; but it can also be used in the figurative sense of providing descendants, as in Deut 25,9; Ru 4,11 *(BNH bayit)*; Exod 1,21 *('ŚH bāttîm)*. It would seem that here neither sense can be excluded. *lō' b^eqārôb*, which is only found here in the MT, adds further possibilities to the interpretation of the first part of the quotation. *qārôb* might be interpreted in a personal sense as a reference to close relatives. This combines nicely with the figurative sense of *b^enôt bāttîm* so that the whole may be seen as a prohibition of marriage with close relations[60]. But Ezekiel would hardly cite such a command as part of a quotation he intends to refute[61]. *b^eqārôb* might also be interpreted spatially, by analogy with *b^erāḥôq* in Ps 10,1. The actual activity of these men might then be similar to the accumulation of property by those reprimanded in Mic 2,2 and Isa 5,8: they intend to build as far as they like in their unrestrained greed for property. Thus one might render: "Do not build houses only in the vicinity!" However, the vagueness of *b^eqārôb* interpreted thus makes this rendering also doubtful. It is when *qārôb* is taken in a temporal sense that the most lucid interpretation is forthcoming. As such it could refer to past or future time. With a reference to past time one might render the phrase as a statement: "Houses have not recently been built". More convincingly, it might be rendered as a complacent rhetorical question: "Have not the houses recently been rebuilt?" (thus the LXX and Vg). But temporal *qārôb* in Ezekiel always refers to the future (7,7.8; 30,3), and the second part of the quotation shows that their future prosperity is the pressing concern of these men. Thus a suitable literal rendering would be "Houses will not be built up soon". Such a statement could well be an expression of despair, but the confidence shown in the second part of the quotation and the harsh reply given to the quotation in the refutations indicate that this first part too is an expression of the speakers' arrogance and complacency.

---

[60] Thus HORST, "Exilsgemeinde", 340.
[61] ZIMMERLI, *Ezechiel*, 244.

Thus the sense of what the leaders are saying is: "We have plenty of time to build up the houses". A rendering as a rhetorical question, "Won't the houses soon be rebuilt ?" is also possible, but this would more probably be introduced by *hᾰlô'*. The reading proposed here allows the double meaning of "house": they are as smugly complacent about the building of houses as they are about the firm establishment of their families as the new ruling dynasties. They have asserted their control sufficiently and are cock-sure about their continuing power in the city. The phrase thus expresses similar sentiments to those shown in the proverb "Rome was not built in a day!"

The second half of the quotation, "this is the pot and we are the meat", also has no parallels in the MT. In Jer 1,13 and Mic 3,3 the cooking pot symbolises disaster and oppression in two different ways. In Ezek 24,3.6 the pot is the city about to be destroyed. But here the pot is a protective shield for the leaders in Jerusalem, the meat safe inside, as is made clear in the refutations.

Preparatory Remarks

4   And so, prophesy against them, prophesy,
         son of man!
5   And the Spirit of Yahweh overcame me,
         and he said to me: Speak! Thus says Yahweh:
         You speak thus, house of Israel,
         and I know the thoughts of your hearts.
6   You have multiplied your victims in this city,
         and filled its streets with victims.

    yᵉdaᶜtîhᾱ is to be read *yᵉdaᶜtî* (dittography).

Further words of Yahweh come between the quotation and the refutation. In Jer 33,24b such additional words were called an "explanatory remark" since they gave further clarity to the quotation of the people. Yahweh's words in Ezek 11,4-6 look forward rather than back and prepare for the refutations. Yahweh first encourages the prophet to speak in vv.4-5a. A narrative parenthesis in v.5a announces the coming of the Spirit. With the words "you speak thus, house of Israel" in v.5a Yahweh refers directly to the quotation of the rulers' words. He knows the plans which lie behind such arrogant assertions. V.6 lastly has the important task of introducing the term *ḥᾱlᾱl*, which will be central to the first refutation. These *ḥᾱlᾱl* are the victims of judicial murder, who have fallen at the hands of the new rulers[62]. Yahweh knows that the rulers

---

[62] EISSFELDT, "Schwerterschlagene", 73-81, shows how *ḥᾱlᾱl* in Ezekiel does not refer exclusively to those slain in war. Thus there is no need to consider v.6 as containing a threat for the future, as do ZIMMERLI, *Ezechiel*, 245, and HORST, "Exilsgemeinde", 341.

intend to eliminate unwanted people through judicial murder, and that they have already put this plan into action.

The Refutations

The first part of the quotation is not explicitly refuted, but there are two separate refutations in which v.3b is contradicted, and in two different ways, as shown by v.7 and v.11. Each refutation concludes with the formula of recognition of Yahweh, briefly in v.10, and in an extended form in v.12. The only irregularity in the formal structure of the two refutations is the lack of a formal introduction to the second refutation in v.11, but this in no way invalidates the basic division of the text[63].

First Refutation

7   And so, thus says the Lord Yahweh:
        The victims you have gathered inside it,
        they are the meat and this is the pot.
        But you I will take out of it.
8   You fear the sword,
        so I will bring the sword against you,
        it is the Lord Yahweh who speaks.
9   And I will take you out of it,
        and give you into the hands of foreigners,
        and I will pass judgements upon you.
10   You will fall by the sword.
        I will judge you in the territory of Israel.
        And you will know that I am Yahweh.

            In v.7 *hôṣî'* is to be read *'ôṣî'*.

In the first refutation of v.3b Ezekiel allows the statement that the city is the pot to pass. But he challenges the leaders' claim to be the meat. They regard themselves as meat of high quality, well protected by the pot, but Ezekiel uncannily reinterprets this meat to refer to the corpses of the people they have

---

[63] ZIMMERLI, *Ezechiel*, 245, takes vv.6-8 together as an announcement of coming judgement, misinterpreting v.6 and undervaluing the new beginning in v.7. V.6 in fact helps to explain the thoughts referred to in v.5, so the verses must be taken together. The formula *n^e'um 'ădōnāy yhwh* at the end of v.8 does not conclude the section, but lays stress on Yahweh's word in the middle of the first refutation. Zimmerli is thus driven to consider vv.9-12 an addition. The clear structure of two refutations, beginning with challenges to the quotation in v.7 and v.11, and ending with the concluding formulae in v.10 and v.12, argues strongly against such a division.

done away with according to their evil plans, the *ḥālāl* of v.6. It is they who are the meat within the pot. Ezekiel must then account for the fate of the leaders. This he does in vv.7b-10 with the insistent *'etkem* (four times), *'ălêkem* and *bākem*. They will meet their judgement outside the safety of the city by the swords of foreigners.

The expression *'al- ('el-) gᵉbûl yiśrā'ēl* in vv.10.11 is often rendered "on the border of Israel"[64]. This is understood as a reference to Nebuchadnezzar's judgements upon the leading men of Judah at Riblah (2 Kgs 25,18-21), and the material is considered a later addition[65]. *gᵉbûl yiśrā'ēl*, however, in the overwhelming majority of cases, refers not to the border of Israel, but to its territory[66]. The sense thus obtained, "I will judge you in the territory of Israel", serves as a contrast to the fate of the exiles outside Israel, which will be the concern of Ezek 11,14-17[67].

Second Refutation

11   It will no longer be a pot for you,
        but you will be meat inside it.
        I will judge you in the territory of Israel.
12   And you will know that I am Yahweh,
        for you have not walked in my statutes,
        you have not kept my commandments,
        you have followed the commandments
        of the nations around you.

In the second refutation of v.3b Ezekiel by contrast with the first refutation declares that the city will no longer be a pot to protect the rulers, but that they will indeed be meat. But he has already given his own interpretation of "meat" in v.7, and the leaders are destined to become meat of this sort. Translations and commentaries interpret both clauses in v.11a as negative, following the lead of the LXX[68]. Although such a rendering is possible, it is more satisfactory to interpret the waw as marking a contrast, so that the second clause is positive. In this way v.11 provides a most effective climax in the disputation speech: the

---

[64] *RSV*: "I will judge you at the border of Israel." ZIMMERLI: "An der Grenze Israels will ich euch richten."

[65] Thus BERTHOLET, *Hesekiel*, 34; COOKE, *Ezekiel*, 123; ZIMMERLI, *Ezechiel*, 245; EICHRODT, *Hesekiel*, 49, n. 2; WEVERS, *Ezekiel*, 92.

[66] OTTOSSON, "*gᵉbûl*", 899, lists the occurrences, finding only 2 Kgs 14,25 to refer to the border of the northern kingdom.

[67] *TOB* gives the correct rendering: "je vous jugerai sur le territoire même d'Israël".

[68] *RSV*: "This city shall not be your cauldron, nor shall you be the flesh in the midst of it." *TOB*: "La ville ne sera pas pour vous une marmite et vous n'y serez pas la viande." ZIMMERLI: "Sie soll euch nicht zum Topf werden, so dass ihr zum Fleisch darin würdet."

reinterpretation of "meat" by Ezekiel in v.7 allows him to deliver the final blow here. The leaders will indeed be meat, but the meat of a slain corpse[69].

The second refutation is characterised by *tihyeh* and *tihyû* which refer to the future, while the quotation itself and the first refutation when it begins in v.7 refer to the present. The cooking pot may afford protection now, but there will come a time when it will no longer do so. The victims of judicial murder are the corpses of today, but the speakers of the quotation will be the corpses of tomorrow. By contrast to the exiles these men will be judged within Israel; the city will not protect them; they will indeed become the meat[70].

Thus Ezekiel challenges the quotation in two different ways: he first allows the city to be the pot, but denies that the speakers of the quotation are the meat; and secondly denies that the city will be a pot to protect them, allowing them to be meat in quite a different way. The double refutation of the quotation thus grows in strength, finally denying the protective role of the city and declaring the speakers of the quotation to be meat in a sense they never expected. This clever rejection of the quotation in two stages shows the unity of vv.2-12 within the framework of v.1 and v.13.

Conclusion

The disputation speech in vv.2-12 refutes the assertions of those who have taken power by force after the departure of the exiles. Ezekiel's dire predictions of coming disaster for them are underlined in the concluding part of the vision in v.13 with the narration of the sudden death of Pelatiah. This disputation speech is unique in being located within a vision. The minor vision of vv.1-13 is in turn set in the major vision of Ezek 8-11. Both visions announce judgement against those in Jerusalem, one in a vision narrative, the other by challenging the new rulers' confident assertions in a disputation speech.

Ezekiel 11,14-17

Context, Structure and Unity

Like Ezek 11,2-12, this disputation speech takes as its starting point words

---

[69] COOKE, *Ezekiel*, 127, while admitting that the negative may sometimes affect two clauses, holds that this is hardly such a case. He therefore inserts a second negative in order to maintain the usual translation.

[70] Translating "you will be meat inside it" in v.11a does produce a certain tension between "inside it", namely the city, and "in the territory of Israel" in v.11b, if this latter is interpreted as outside the city in conformity with the first refutation (vv.7b.9a). One might venture the reply that Ezekiel already considered these men to be condemned as corpses in the city regardless of where they would eventually bite the dust. The refutations taken separately are consistent; the tension here arises perhaps from an over-precise consideration of Ezekiel's invective.

attributed to those left in Jerusalem. The refutation, however, challenges their
claim not with the announcement of coming judgement upon them, but by
reference to Yahweh's continuing care for the exiles, which will lead eventually
to their return to the land. The disputation speech lies parallel to 11,2-12, showing the hopeful future for the exiles as a contrast to the calamity in store for
those in Jerusalem. It also provides an answer to Ezekiel's question to God in
v.13, "Ah, Lord Yahweh, will you totally destroy the remnant of Israel?" Unlike
the preceding disputation speech, 11,14-17 is not set within a vision, though the
redactor has placed it within the major vision of Ezek 8-11.

The disputation speech has two refutations introduced by the formulae in
v.16 and v.17. V.16 refers to the exiles in the third person, but v.17 is directed to
them as "you". Vv.18-20 then strangely refer to them once more in the third
person, with the exception of b^eqirb^ekem in v.19. Light can be shed on this
perplexing confusion of pronouns by reference to the disputation speech in
Ezek 33,23-29. After the initial quotation of words spoken by those left in
Jerusalem there are two refutations, both introduced by formulae in v.25 and
v.27. Both refutations concern those left in Jerusalem, but the first addresses
the speakers of the quotations directly as "you", whereas the second refers to
them in the third person. Although the whole speech, like Ezek 11,14-17, is to be
understood as actually delivered to the exiles, the grammatical addressee after
the introductory formulae changes from those in Jerusalem in the first refutation in vv.25-26 to those in the exile in the second refutation in vv.27-29. A
similar process in seen in Ezek 11,16-17. Whereas the first refutation in v.16 is
directed grammatically to those who spoke the quotation and thus refers to the
exiles in the third person, in the second refutation in v.17 the exiles are addressed directly in the second person. The difference between 11,16-17 and 33,25-29
is that the refutations in Ezek 11 concern the exiles' future, whereas those in
Ezek 33 announce the fate of those in Jerusalem. Nevertheless, in both disputation speeches the first refutation is grammatically addressed to the speakers of
the quotation back in Jerusalem, while the second is directed to the actual
listeners in the exile.

The fact that in Ezek 11,18-20 the speech reverts to the third person for the
exiles suggests that these verses are an addition[71]. V.21 in its turn has been ap-
pended to v.20 to give an admonitory conclusion to the disputation speech. The
two original refutations are v.16 and v.17. They are of similar length, whereas

---

[71] An exact parallel to Ezek 11,19-20 is to be found in Ezek 36,26-28, with extra material in
vv.27a.28a. This text is shown to be an addition by SIMIAN, *Die theologische Nachgeschichte*, 91-92, a
further indication that 11,19-20 could well be an addition. V.18 must be considered a linking verse. A
different solution is proposed by ZIMMERLI, *Ezechiel*, 200-201,249. He takes the verses using the third
person for the exiles as his basic text, vv.16.19.20. He rejects v.18 as a later addition to v.17. This
however ignores the formulae which show the structure of two refutations. Zimmerli's basic text also
implies that the new heart would be bestowed in the exile, a point which would contradict the tradition found again in Ezek 36, and also in Jer 32,37-41.

an acceptance of vv.18-20 as part of the original speech would have produced a strange disproportion in the lengths of the two refutations.

Introduction

14   The word of Yahweh came to me saying:
15   Son of man,
        your brothers, your kinsmen,
        and the whole house of Israel,
        it is about them that the inhabitants
        of Jerusalem are talking when they say:

The formula of the coming of the word introduces the disputation speech. V.15 begins by mentioning as three groups the exiles about whom the inhabitants of Jerusalem have coined their saying. The three groups are suspended in the sentence as a "casus pendens", made more awkward by the following relative pronoun.

The repetition of "your brothers" is hard to justify, coming as it does in this list of three categories. There seems no reason for Ezekiel to lay particular stress on his brothers as distinct from the others. It is best therefore to consider this a case of dittography[72].

The second group, "your kinsmen", widens the horizon from Ezekiel's brothers. It designates all those who would be able, due to close relationship, to exercise the right of redemption on the property of the prophet. The expression, literally "men of your redemption", serves to introduce the idea of possession of property which is the object of the claim expressed in the quotation. This expression is only found here, but the theme of redemption of land is frequent in the OT (Jer 32,7-8; Lev 25,24.26; Ru 4,6-7)[73].

The final category of those spoken about widens the view still further to all the exiles. Since the words of the quotation refer to all those who have gone far from Yahweh into exile, this third category is necessary to complete the picture and should not be considered additional[74].

---

[72] ZIMMERLI, *Ezechiel*, 200, maintains the text as it stands with the sense "all your brothers". Similar repetitions of plural forms found in GKC 123 e, however, lay far greater stress on the great number of objects concerned, as in Judg 5,22; Exod 8,10; Joel 4,14. EICHRODT, *Hesekiel*, 49, n. 4, is correct in considering the repetition out of place here.

[73] The uniqueness of the expression "men of your redemption" has led to the suggested correction to *gālûtekā*. Thus HOELSCHER, *Hesekiel*, 77, n. 2; BERTHOLET, *Hesekiel*, 40; COOKE, *Ezechiel*, 127; FOHRER, *Ezechiel*, 61; EICHRODT, *Hesekiel*, 49, n. 5. On the other hand, ZIMMERLI, *Ezechiel*, 190, renders "deine Sippenangehörigen". WEVERS, *Ezechiel*, 96, too prefers "men of your kindred". The interpretation, "the men banished with you", would destroy the gradual progression from "your brothers" to "the whole house of Israel". Furthermore the exiles are usually simply *haggôlâ* in Ezekiel and the only instance of *galût* with a suffix is with the first person plural suffix in 33,21 and 40,1.

[74] This final category is considered an addition by HOELSCHER, *Hesekiel*, 77, n. 2; FOHRER. *Ezechiel*, 61; EICHRODT, *Hesekiel*, 49. n. 6.

It is those left in Jerusalem who speak the coming words, or at least have such words attributed to them by the prophet.

Quotation

15   They have gone far from Yahweh;
          it is to us that the land has been given
          as our property.
             raḥăqû is to be read *rāḥăqû*.

The exiles' going far from Yahweh has a double sense. The idea of physical separation from the sanctuary of Yahweh will be taken up again in Yahweh's first reply in v.16. But the phrase also has a moral sense, seen again in reference to the Levites who abandoned Yahweh in Ezek 44,10. A similar use of *RḤQ* is found in Jer 2,5. This twofold departure from Yahweh by the exiles allows the citizens of Jerusalem to claim the land for themselves.

The phrase *NTN (lᵉ) môrāšâ* is used for the wholesale surrender of land by one people to another in Ezek 25,4.10; 36,5 and Exod 6,8. Thus it is inferred here that the exiles are already an alien people. Since God is the usual subject of the phrase (Ezek 25,4.10; Exod 6,8), the use of the niphal in this case may well imply that the land has been ceded to those dwelling in Jerusalem by divine decree.

The quotation thus contains a claim to the land on two counts. It is a legal claim to possession due to the departure from the land of the previous owners who are not expected to return. But it is also a religious claim: the previous owners have abandoned Yahweh, who has therefore granted the land to a new people. The quotation thus loads all guilt on the shoulders of the exiles.

As is usual in disputation speeches, the quotation is quite true to life. The fact that Jeremiah makes no mention of such early claims to the land by those remaining in Jerusalem should not be used to cast doubt on the likelihood of such claims[75]. Neither should the similarity of the quotation with that in 33,24 be used to situate 11,15 with that quotation after the destruction of Jerusalem[76]. The similarity of expression amounts only to four words in the Hebrew text, the actual claim of possession of the land. The difference in description of the speakers of the quotation is more significant, for in 33,24 they will be called "inhabitants of those ruins".

---

[75] ZIMMERLI, *Ezechiel*, 251, suggests the quotation may have been invented by the exiles due to their feeling of despair and of being forgotten.
[76] Thus EICHRODT, *Hesekiel*, 74.

The Refutations

Once more there are two replies to the quotation, as in Ezek 11,2-12. In that disputation speech the quotation was tackled in two different ways, and whereas the first refutation referred to the contemporary situation the second looked to the future. In Ezek 11,16-17 the two refutations also succeed each other in chronological order, v.16 referring to the past and present, and v.17 looking to the future. The first refutation in v.16 admits that the exiles have "gone far", but Yahweh is still close to them. In the second refutation in v.17 the claim to the land is refuted. Thus, while the first refutation contests the first part of the quotation and the assertion of those in Jerusalem that the exiles have gone far from Yahweh, the climax is reached in the second refutation in v.17 when the claim to the land of those in Jerusalem is rejected. The exiles have not in fact been abandoned by Yahweh, and the land will eventually be theirs.

First Refutation

16   Therefore say: thus says the Lord Yahweh:
        I did indeed take them far off among the nations,
        I did indeed scatter them in other lands,
        but I have become a sanctuary for them for a
        while in the lands where they have gone.

The first refutation addresses the speakers of the quotation directly and takes up the verb *RḤQ* from the first part of the quotation. Yahweh has indeed taken them far off, but he intends to be present among them as their sanctuary "for a while". This expression is unique and indicates a real but temporary presence of Yahweh among the exiles[77]. Yahweh's presence will be "for a while", for there will soon be an end to the exile, as the second refutation announces.

Second Refutation

17   Therefore say: thus says the Lord Yahweh:
        I will bring you back from the peoples,
        and I will gather you from the lands

---

[77] $m^{e\,c}a\underline{t}$ in a temporal sense fits better in this context. $m^{e\,c}a\underline{t}$ might be given a qualitative sense as in *TOB*: "j'ai été un peu pour eux un sanctuaire". This is often seen as a reference to the limited observance of the cult possible in the conditions of the exile. Thus EICHRODT, *Hesekiel*, 76. This seems to overemphasise what may be a secondary implication here.

where you have been scattered,
and I will give the land of Israel to you.

The second refutation looks forward to the end of the period of waiting.
The promise of return is delivered directly to the exiles. They will be gathered
from the nations. It is to them that Yahweh will give the land. "I will give the
land of Israel to you" stands in marked contrast to the words of the second part
of the quotation, "it is to us that the land has been given" (v.15b). This final
statement provides a fitting close to the disputation speech.

Conclusion

As in Ezek 11,2-12, there is a chronological sequence between the two
refutations in this disputation speech. At the same time the first refutation
takes up the first part of the quotation, and the second lays greatest stress on
challenging the second part.

The disputation speech serves to counterbalance the announcement of
disaster for those in Jerusalem with a promise of a bright future for the exiles.
Unlike 11,2-12 it has been inserted in the major vision of Ezek 8-11 with no attempt to camouflage the speech as a vision. These two disputation speeches
must make it clear to the despairing exiles before the destruction of Jerusalem
that the future lies not with the unscrupulous new rulers back in Israel, but
with them. This disputation speech explicitly introduces the question of rivalry
for the possession of the land between those left behind and those banished, a
question which will arise again in another disputation speech, Ezek 33,23-29.

Ezekiel 12,21-25

Context and Structure

Two short disputation speeches are found in Ezek 12,21-25.26-28, following
the account of two symbolic actions concerning the coming disaster in
12,1-16.17-20. These two disputation speeches raise the question of the lack of
fulfilment of prophecy and also prepare the way for Ezekiel's attack on the
false prophets in Ezek 13. Though brief, both units show the basic disputation
speech structure complete with formulae.

Introduction

21   The word of Yahweh came to me saying:
22   Son of man,

what is this proverb you have in the land
of Israel which says:

The formula of the coming of the word introduces the speech, as often happens in Ezekiel. The immediate introduction to the quotation is in the form of a question of Yahweh to the prophet, as happens also in Ezek 18,2 and Jer 33,24. The use of a rhetorical question gives the introduction an indignant tone.

The designation of the coming quotation as *māšāl* is not surprising given the wide variety of uses of this term. What is surprising is that the term is found only here (vv.22.23) and in Ezek 18,2.3 in all the disputation speeches. Could it be that the prophets avoided giving ordinary sayings status by designating them *māšāl*? This could well imply that the sayings quoted in Ezek 12,22 and 18,2 were well established proverbs, an idea which in the case of 18,2 is confirmed by the presence of the same proverb in Jer 31,29.

The quotation is described as *ʿal-ʾadmat yiśrāʾel*, which might mean "concerning the land of Israel" or "in the land of Israel". The presence of the same phrase in Ezek 18,2 and particularly in Ezek 33,24, where the quotation referred to is explicitly attributed to those still living in Jerusalem, leads to the choice of the latter phrase, which also fits better with "in Israel" in v.23. Furthermore, it is hard to see how the quotation given here can be described as "concerning the land of Israel"[78].

This first disputation speech, in vv.21-25, is thus concerned with the opinion expressed by, or at least attributed to, those left behind in Jerusalem, in contrast to the disputation speech in vv.26-28, which will concern itself with words of the exiles.

Quotation

22   Many days pass,
          and every vision comes to nothing?

The term *ḥāzôn* used here has come to refer to the message received in a vision, rather than the actual vision[79]. *ʾBD* employed here as often in a figurative sense permits two interpretations. Jer 18,18 states that the word from the prophet, together with the law from the priest and the counsel from the wise man, "will not perish", even if plots are made against Jeremiah. Both this text and Ezek 12,22 could refer to the question of the continuance of pro-

---

[78] HERNTRICH, *Ezechielprobleme*, 99, and BERTHOLET, *Hesekiel*, 44, defend the rendering "in the land of Israel", which is also given by ZIMMERLI, *Ezechiel*, 274, 275.

[79] FUHS, *Sehen*, 234-235. He also points out that, while the value of the *ḥāzôn* is affirmed in v.23, the overall stress of the passage lies on the word of Yahweh. Fuhs speaks of a retreat from conventional vision language and a reinterpretation to give greater emphasis to the word of Yahweh.

phetic activity as such. In this case the Ezekiel quotation might be rendered:
"The days are passing, and all visions will cease." But a second meaning is
possible in both texts, that of individual prophecies losing validity or coming to
nothing. The issue raised is not the possible end of all prophetic visions, but the
lack of fulfilment of prophecies long since announced. Deut 18,21-22 states that
a prophecy can be seen not to come from Yahweh if it remains unfulfilled. The
people have this principle in mind as they comment on the many days which
pass without anything happening.

It is remarkable that the only two disputation speech quotations designated
mašal can be substantiated by reference to Scripture. The quotation in Ezek
18,2 can find support in Exod 34,7 and Num 14,18, while that in Ezek 12,22 can
rely on Deut 18,21-22. What happens in the quotation here is that the people use
Deut 18,21-22 to discredit the prophecies of disaster they have heard. Days are
passing with no fulfilment of such dire predictions; the conclusion must be
drawn that those who made such predictions were not prophets sent by
Yahweh.

Whereas the quotations in Ezek 11,3 and 11,15 showed the confidence of
those in Jerusalem in the face of a desperate political situation, the words in
12,22 show their overriding optimism in spite of prophetic predictions of calamity. Ezekiel himself had announced the nearness of the day of doom quite explicitly in 7,7. The quotation here is a direct challenge to similar declarations
back in Israel, predictions which had not as yet been realised.

Refutation

23   And so, say to them: thus says the Lord Yahweh:
        I have put an end to this proverb;
        they will no longer use it in Israel.
        Rather, say to them:
        The days are approaching,
        and every vision will come true.
24   For there will no longer be any empty visions
        and pleasing divinations in the house of Israel.
25   For I, Yahweh, speak,
        the word I speak comes true,
        it will no longer be delayed.
        Indeed, in your days, house of rebellion,
        I will speak a word and I will fulfil it,
        it is the Lord Yahweh who speaks.

Yahweh announces an end to the use of this proverb in Israel, as he does
again in Ezek 18,3, and substitutes a new proverb for the old in v.23. Ezekiel

uses the pattern found in the disputation speech Jer 31,29-30, *lō' 'MR (MŠL) ʿôd ... kî 'im ...*, to introduce the new proverb, though here by contrast it only provides part of the refutation. The new proverb is a clever adaptation of the people's words. The rhyme and rhythm are the same as in the old proverb, the key words *yāmîm* and *ḥāzôn* return, but the general sense of the yiqtol of *'RK* in v.22 is replaced by the qatal of *QRB* with its specific reference to the present moment. The days are indeed approaching and the calamities announced by the visions of disaster[80].

In v.24 Ezekiel concedes that to some extent the speakers of the quotation are justified. For they have heard many prophecies, some of which have merely been "empty visions" and "pleasing divinations". Ezekiel admits the existence of false prophecies which have contributed to the coining of the proverb in an attempt to weed out the false from the true. Ezekiel will elaborate on the activity of these false prophets in the following chapter with a frequent use of the phrase *ḤZH šāw'* (13,6.7.9.23; also in 21,34; 22,28 and Lam 2,14). *miqsam ḥālāq*, a "smooth" divination, seems to refer to prophecies of peace announced chiefly to put people at their ease; the expression is only found here, though Isa 30,10 has the people ask the prophets for *ḥālāqôt* in a similar context of false prophecy. Such false prophecies will be heard no more. It is quite natural for Ezekiel to announce the end of false prophecy in the house of Israel at this point, since this phenomenon quite certainly aggravated the problem of the slow fulfilment of genuine prophecy, allowing genuine prophets to be considered no better than false ones if their prophecies were not swiftly fulfilled[81]. The internal structure of the refutation also indicates that v.24 is an integral part of the refutation. Just as Yahweh announces in v.23 that a new proverb is to replace the old, so the false prophecies of v.24 are replaced by the word of Yahweh, which comes true, as v.25 announces.

In v.25 Yahweh declares that his word will be realised; there will be no more delay in its fulfilment. The relative clause *'ăšer 'ădabbēr* is to be taken with the following *dābār* as in v.28b, showing that a break is to be made after the first *'ădabbēr*. *'ēt* here marks *dābār*, preceded by the relative clause, as the subject of the coming verb, as in Ezek 17,21 and 35,10[82]. The second part of the

---

[80] The presence of *ûdᵉbar* in v.23b and the lack of a verb parallel to *wᵉ'ābad* in the original quotation led HERRMANN, *Ezechiel*, 78, to propose *ûbā'* as the correct reading. This proposal might be supported by the use of the verb *BW'* in the similar contexts of Deut 18,22 and Jer 28,9. BERTHOLET, *Hesekiel*, 44; FOHRER, *Ezechiel*, 67, and EICHRODT, *Hesekiel*, 79, n. 2, propose *wᵉgābar* should be read. But the lack of another similar use of *GBR*, and the prominence of *dābār* in the disputation speech suggest that the text should be maintained as it stands.

[81] FOHRER, *Ezechiel*, 67, considers vv.24-25a to be a later addition introducing the subject of false prophecy. HOSSFELD, MEYER, *Prophet gegen Prophet*, 122-123, take the same view of v.24: false prophecy is introduced as an excuse for the delay in fulfilment of prophecies.

[82] On *'ēt* marking the subject see JOÜON, *Grammaire*, 125 j, and BROCKELMANN, *Syntax*, 31 b. On the preceding relative clause see GKC 138 e. ZIMMERLI, *Ezechiel*, 274-275, sees the waw before *yᵉ'āśeh* to be quite acceptable since the sentence has a temporal-conditional nuance.

verse stresses with the emphatic *kî* that the fulfilment will come "in your days". The whole of v.25 is dominated by the root *DBR* which occurs five times. It is the word which is effective, and precisely because it comes from Yahweh its fulfilment will not be delayed. The niphal use of *MŠK* is found again in Isa 13,22 in a similar sense: the days before the fulfilment of the prediction will be quickly over.

Conclusion

In this disputation speech the inhabitants of Jerusalem take advantage of the failure in fulfilment of prophecies of disaster in order to mock the prophets. Their attack is made more biting by their being able to quote Scripture to support their stand. They thus endeavour to dismiss awkward prophecies and avoid facing up to their implications. In reply Ezekiel proposes no new solution to the problem of the delay. While announcing an end to false prophecy, he reiterates that Yahweh's word will be fulfilled, and fulfilled soon. The people are simply called upon to believe him; when his word is fulfilled they will know he is a true prophet (33,33). For the time being the only solution is to believe that this prophet is indeed sent by Yahweh[83].

Ezekiel 12,26-28

Introduction

26   And the word of Yahweh came to me saying:
27   Son of man,
        the house of Israel are saying:

The second of this pair of disputation speeches is also introduced by the formula of the coming of the word. The speakers of the coming quotation are the house of Israel, which the context shows to refer to the exiles, for they will comment on what "he", the prophet who lives among them, preaches.

Quotation

27   The vision he sees is for distant days,
        for far-off times he prophesies.

---

[83] EICHRODT, *Hesekiel*, 85, 100.

The quotation shows a clear chiastic structure, as do other disputation speech quotations in Ezek 33,24; Isa 40,27 and 49,14. As in Ezek 12,22, the message is referred to as *ḥāzôn*. This quotation, however, is not a general challenge to unfulfilled prophetic words, but deals with the unfulfilled words of Ezekiel, saying that they will be realised only in the distant future. Once again the quotation concerns the lack of fulfilment of prophecies, but this quotation has a less aggressive tone.

Refutation

28   And so say to them: thus says the Lord Yahweh:
        They will no longer be delayed, all my words;
        the word which I speak comes true,
        it is the Lord Yahweh who speaks.

The refutation, after the introductory formulae, uses certain elements of the final verse of the previous refutation in 12,25. No new quotation is offered here, no allusion is made to false prophecies. The essential answer is that Yahweh's word will soon be fulfilled; there will be no more delay in the realisation of any of his words. The presence of similar phrases to those found in the previous disputation speech does not logically lead to the conclusion that the section is redactional repetition[84]. It simply indicates that a similar problem is being faced. Ezekiel must reiterate the message that Yahweh's word will come true.

It is not clear at first sight whether this disputation speech concerns Ezekiel's prophecies of disaster or his promises for the future[85]. The identical expression "vision for distant days" in Dan 8,26 sheds little light on the quotation. But the milder tone of the disputation speech by contrast to vv.21-25 suggests that Ezekiel's promises of a better future, such as that found in 11,17, may well be concerned. In the introduction to this disputation speech no rhetorical question expresses Yahweh's dismay at the words of the quotation. The refutation does not stress the end of the use of the saying in the house of Israel. Furthermore, it cannot be denied that Ezekiel's promises of salvation would be just as important to those in Babylon as his prophecies about the fate of those remaining in Jerusalem. The tone of the quotation and refutation makes it more likely that the quotation is an expression of despondency at the delay in fulfilment of Ezekiel's promises of a coming improvement in the for-

---

[84] Thus KUHL, "Die 'Wiederaufnahme'", 8-9.
[85] It is usual to refer the speech, like 12,21-25, to prophecies of the destruction of Jerusalem, even though the quotation arises among the exiles. Thus ZIMMERLI, *Ezechiel*, 279-280, and EICHRODT, *Hesekiel*, 85-86.

tunes of the exiles. The refutation then encourages the people by saying that the word from Yahweh will indeed soon come true.

Conclusion

This disputation speech, though it has so much in common with 12,21-25 and lies alongside it, is of a different tone. The prophet assures the exiles, who express their despair that his prophecies are not being fulfilled, that the words will soon be realised. What unites both disputation speeches is the stress they lay on Yahweh's word: it will not fail; whether for good or evil, the word announced by the prophets of Yahweh will soon be fulfilled.

Ezekiel 18,1-20

Context, Structure and Unity

Ezek 18,1-32 is inserted between Ezek 17 and Ezek 19, breaking the flow of allegorical material with a disputation speech in a formal, legal style[86].

It is, however, the question of the unity of the speech which is of primary concern. Ezek 18,1-18 displays the structure of a disputation speech with introduction, quotation and refutation. But the disputation speech is extended. In v.19a the people speak again and question the prophet on what he has said, and he addresses them again in vv.19b-20. This addition of two extra elements, the "rejoinder" and the "reply", will be found also in the closely related disputation speech, Ezek 33,10-20, where there are two rejoinders and two replies in vv.17-20.

Ezek 18,21-32, on the other hand, introduces a quite different issue. Whereas in vv.1-20 the prophet contests the people's proverb in v.2 and illustrates by reference to individuals of three successive generations how each receives the rewards of his own conduct, vv.21-32 introduce the separate issue of the possibility of change for better or worse within the life of the individual. Conversion from evil to good will mean he is rewarded with life; perversion from good to evil will lead to his death. This latter material is found again in 33,11-20, where it comes as a direct answer to the quotation of the people in 33,10. This quotation expresses despair since the people feel they can do nothing to remedy their desperate situation. It is in 33,11-20 that the material concerning the possibility of change in the life of an individual fits better as a reply to the quotation in v.10. By reforming their lives they can change their

---

[86] ZIMMERLI, *Ezechiel*, 110*, suggests it is inserted here due to the judgement on a succession of kings announced in both Ezek 17 and Ezek 19. Ezek 18 too deals with judgement on a succession of individuals.

future. In Ezek 18,21-32, on the other hand, the material is a later addition, the purpose of which is to counterbalance the preceding verses by showing that, although each man does suffer for his own sin, it is always possible for a man to reform his life[87].

Futhermore, 33,10-20 is closely related to 33,1-9, where the prophet is given the task of watchman to instruct the people to change their lives. ŠWB, first introduced in v.9, will dominate the disputation speech in vv.10-20. Thus both content and structure indicate that 18,1-20 and 33,10-20 are the two original units, two disputation speeches, dealing with separate though related issues. Both display the additional elements of rejoinder and reply. The inclusion in 18,4b.20a gives further weight to this analysis, marking 18,1-20 as an extended disputation speech[88].

This disputation speech also displays another new element, the programmatic refutation in vv.3-4, a device found again in Ezek 20,33; 33,11; Isa 49,15 and Hag 1,4. It is a concise rejection of the quotation which prepares for the lengthy explanation to come in the refutation proper. The refutation itself has three sections, corresponding to the three generations dealt with, in vv.5-9.10-13 and 14-18.

Introduction

1   And the word of Yahweh came to me, saying:
2   Why are you repeating this proverb
         in the land of Israel, saying:

   The formula of the coming of the word introduces the unit. A question is addressed to the prophet regarding the proverb, as in Ezek 12,22 and Jer 33,24. As in Ezek 12,22, the words of the people are termed *māšāl*, indicating a well established proverb. *ʿal-'admat yiśrā'ēl*, as in Ezek 12,22 and 33,24, is to be rendered "in the land of Israel"[89].

---

[87] Ezek 18,21-32 rearranges the material from 33,11-20 in order to mention first the possibility of change from evil to good which leads to the reward of life. The awkward interruption in the presentation of the two cases of conversion and perversion produced by v.23, which corresponds to the beginning of the refutation in 33,10-20, is noted by ZIMMERLI, *Ezechiel*, 413. It can be explained by the realisation that material originally found in 33,10-20 has here been rearranged. DEL OLMO LETE, "Ez. 33,1-20", 31, notes that the order of the parts in 33,10-20 runs more smoothly.

[88] ZIMMERLI, *Ezechiel*, 396, uses the unity of 33,10-20, which he rightly defends against Fohrer, as an argument against making a break at 18,20, although he admits that 18,21 introduces a new theme. His claim that vv.1-20 alone would be an academic discussion does not prove the original unity of vv.1-32, as he suggests, but rather explains the later addition of vv.21-32 containing material from 33,10-20.

[89] SCHARBERT, *Solidarität*, 223, n. 369, defends "about the land of Israel" as the correct rendering, and gives the insufficient justification that the prophet is addressing the exiles. The rendering is to be rejected not only due to the parallels, especially Ezek 33,24, but also due to the sense. The quotation is hardly about the land of Israel.

Quotation

2   The fathers eat sour grapes,
           but the teeth of the sons are set on edge?

The quotation is almost identical to that found in Jer 31,29. Ezekiel uses the yiqtol in contrast to Jeremiah's qatal of 'KL, giving the quotation a more general sense; he also adds the article to *bānîm*. These two separate instances, and the presence of similar sentiments in Lam 5,7, show that such feelings were widespread in Israel. As with Ezek 12,22, it is a proverb which can claim scriptural support, this time from texts such as Exod 34,7 and Num 14,18. The people impugn God's justice, refusing to accept guilt and responsibility for the punishment inflicted on them.

Programmatic Refutation

3   As I live, says the Lord Yahweh,
           there will be no more quoting
           of this proverb in Israel.
4   For all persons belong to me,
           the person of the father,
           like the person of the son,
           belongs to me.
           It is the person who sins that shall die.

The programmatic refutation begins with an oath, which announces with greater vigour than in Ezek 12,23 that the proverb will no longer be used. Such oaths are again found in programmatic refutations in Ezek 20,33 and 33,11, and also to begin the second refutation in Ezek 33,27. V.4 provides a concise answer to the quotation, an answer which will be explained in what follows[90]. The presence of the programmatic refutation containing an oath in the related disputation speech, Ezek 33,10-20, is a further indication that the original units are 18,1-20 and 33,10-20. The combination of *nepeš* and *ḤṬ'* is found in priestly law texts such as Lev 4,2.27; 5,1.17.21 and Num 15,27 in reference to a variety of sins. Such priestly expressions are used throughout the refutation.

---

[90] VON RAD, *Theologie*, I, 405, calls v.4 the "counter-thesis". The term "programmatic refutation" is intended to stress that the verse is preparing the detailed explanation in the verses which follow.

Refutation (in three parts)

I

5   If a man is just,
        and acts justly and righteously,
6   he does not eat on the mountains,
        nor raise up his eyes to the idols
        of the house of Israel,
        he does not defile the wife of his neighbour,
        nor approach a woman in her time of impurity,
7   he oppresses no-one,
        he returns the pledge of the debtor,
        he commits no robbery,
        he gives his bread to the hungry man,
        and covers the naked one with clothing,
8   he does not lend at interest,
        nor practise usury,
        he withdraws his hand from evil,
        and gives true judgement between men,
9   he walks in my statutes,
        and keeps my commandments, acting faithfully.
        This man is just: he shall certainly live,
        says the Lord Yahweh.

> In v.7 for ḥăbōlātô ḥôb read ḥăbōl ḥayyāb
> as the LXX.

II

10   This man fathers a violent son who sheds blood,
        who does any one of these things,
11   whereas his father did none of them.
        But he eats on the mountains,
        and defiles the wife of his neighbour,
12   he oppresses the destitute and the poor,
        he commits robberies,
        he does not return the pledge,
        he raises up his eyes to idols,
        he commits abominations,
13   he lends at interest,
        and practises usury.

Should he live?
He shall not live.
He has committed all these abominations.
He shall be put to death.
His blood will be on his own head.

> V.10: omit ʾaḥ, and interpret as Lev
> 4,2; 5,13.

III

14   And now he fathers a son
        who sees all the sins his father has committed,
        he sees and he does not act likewise.
15   He does not eat on the mountains,
        nor raise up his eyes to the idols
        of the house of Israel,
        he does not defile the wife of his neighbour,
16   he oppresses no man,
        he takes no pledge,
        he commits no robbery,
        he gives his bread to the hungry man,
        and covers the naked one with clothing,
17   he withdraws his hand from evil,
        he takes no interest nor practises usury,
        he obeys my commandments and walks in my statutes.
        He will not die for the guilt of his father,
        he shall certainly live.
18   His father, the one who practised violence,
        committed robbery,
        and did what is not good among his people,
        it is he who dies for his own guilt.

> In v.17 meʿanî is to be read meʿawel as
> in v.8.
> In v.18 gēzel ʾaḥ is to be read gᵉzēlâ
> as in v.7 and v.16.

Following the programmatic refutation three cases are presented. In a similar fashion, in 33,10-20, two cases will be considered in the refutation.

The first case here presents the just man with no reference to his parentage. V.5 declares him to be just. Vv.6-8 then give thirteen instances of the conduct of this man, five actions which he performs and eight sins which he is careful to avoid. Whereas the expressions "eat on the mountains" and "raise up one's eyes to idols" are typical of Ezekiel, most of the other activities are mentioned in the codes of the Law, even if in different terms[91]. In v.9, which concludes the first case, the man is declared to be just by the words *ṣaddîq hû'*, which recall similar priestly declarations regarding sacrifices in Lev 1,17 and 2,15. The promise of life for the man concludes the consideration of this first case.

The second case uses the same elements to consider the wicked son of the just father in vv.10-13. The number of actions is reduced. No parallel declaration to *ṣaddîq hû'* in v.9 is found, but the sentence of death is concluded in v.13 by the expression "his blood will be on his own head", a formula similar to that found repeatedly in Lev 20 (vv.9.11.12.13.16.27) in the context of death by execution.

It is only with the third case in vv.14-18 that a direct reply is obtained for the people's complaint that innocent sons suffer due to the guilt of their fathers, for here Ezekiel presents the case of a just son of a wicked father. V.14 stresses the contrast between father and son; v.17 announces that the son will surely live, omitting the declaration *ṣaddîq hû'*. Finally, v.18 makes the message clear by referring back to the evil ways of the father which will bring death to him, and to him alone.

The verses of the refutation display many elements found in legal texts. Concern with successive generations is a priestly trait found in the genealogies. Conditional *kî* in v.5 and v.18 is characteristic of casuistic law. The lists of actions performed or avoided are obvious legal material. All these elements, with the concluding declaration in v.9, the promises of life in vv.9 and 17, and the sentence to death in v.13, show how Ezekiel adopts various aspects of legal usage to give greater authority to his refutation of the people's words[92].

Thus, with these three cases, Ezekiel has shown how each individual will receive the consequences of his actions, and that guilt or merit are not transferred to successive generations. Using elements of the legal language of the priests he has demonstrated the falsity of the quotation.

Rejoinder and Reply

19   You will say:
          Why does not the son suffer

---

[91] For full details of the parallels in particular from the Covenant Code, Deuteronomy and the Holiness Code see ZIMMERLI, *Ezechiel*, 405-406. It is unnecessary to change "eating on the mountains" to the less crucial "eating with blood", as suggested by REVENTLOW, *Wächter*, 109. The change is further dissuaded by the threefold appearance of the phrase, in vv.6.11.15.

[92] ZIMMERLI, *Ezechiel*, 396-400, proposes that these elements are modelled on a rite of admission to the temple performed by the priests for pilgrims. REVENTLOW, *Wächter*, 111-113, lays greater stress on the legal origin especially as regards the promise of life or death. See also SCHULZ, *Das Todesrecht*, 167-178.

         for the guilt of the father?
         The son has acted justly and righteously,
         he has kept all my statutes and performed them.
         He shall certainly live.
20   It is the person who sins that shall die.
         The son shall not suffer for the guilt
         of the father,
         the father shall not suffer for the guilt
         of the son.
         The justice of the just man will rest upon him,
         the wickedness of the wicked man will rest
         upon him.

The people's rejoinder in v.19a and the reply of the prophet extend the disputation speech. The people are reluctant to accept the prophet's explanation, for it means that they can no longer transfer their own guilt to others. This at any rate is how the prophet foresees they might react. They question the prophet and challenge all that he has proposed.

The phrase *NŚᵓ baʿăwōn* is unique in the whole MT to these two verses of Ezekiel. *NŚᵓᶜăwōn* in Ezekiel refers both to the bearing of the consequences of one's own sin (14,10; 44,10.12) or the sin of others (4,4-6). *NŚᵓbaʿăwōn*, however, exclusively denotes the bearing of punishment due to another, a suffering due to the guilt of another[93].

The repetition of the "counter-thesis" denies the people's opinion once more in v.20: "It is the person who sins that shall die." This reply does not penetrate any more deeply into the problem, but reaffirms the point made at greater length by the refutation.

Conclusion

Ezekiel deals with the same quotation of the people in quite a different way from Jeremiah. Whereas Jer 31,29-30 looked forward to future days when the people would see the justice of God's ways and replace their proverb with words affirming God's justice, Ezekiel illustrates in a lengthy casuistic style his fundamental repudiation of the proverb. The aim of the disputation speech is quite simply to contest and refute the quotation, not to introduce the call to conversion in vv.30-32, which is quite a different issue[94]. Nevertheless, the starkness of 18,1-20 plainly invited the addition of more auspicious words inspired principally by 33,10-20.

---

[93] ZIMMERLI, *Ezechiel*, 394-395, suggests this is an instance of *bᵉ*-pretii.
[94] Contrast ZIMMERLI, *Ezechiel*, 415.

Ezekiel 20,32-44

Context, Structure and Unity

Ezekiel 20 has sometimes been considered a unit[95]. The majority of com-
mentators, however, find it necessary to divide the chapter, though opinions
vary as to whether the break should be made after v.31 or after v.32[96]. A close
examination of vv.32-33, however, shows that these two verses constitute the
beginning of a disputation speech. V.32, with its novel introduction, presents a
quotation of the people. V.33 is not only the beginning of a refutation, but contains a programmatic refutation with an oath, as found in both Ezek 18,3-4 and
33,11. These similarities are a strong indication that the break is to be made
before v.32. This is confirmed by the renewed refusal of Yahweh to be con-
sulted by the elders in v.31, which forms an inclusion with v.3 and closes that
unit. The quotation in v.32 is to be considered not as an illustration of the attitude of the elders of v.1, whose request to the prophet has been refused, but
as the beginning of a new unit, which is a disputation speech[97].

The remaining verses of the refutation are divided into three sections,
vv.34-38.39-42.43-44, by the formula of recognition of Yahweh found in
vv.38.42.44[98]. These three sections will illustrate the programmatic refutation
in v.33, and reject the people's view that their future lies in the service of wood
and stone. A further similarity with 18,1-20 is evident in the fact that the programmatic refutation is explained in three stages, though here the future fate
of the house of Israel at present in exile is the theme.

Introduction

32   What you have in mind
        shall certainly not come to pass;
        you say:

The lack of a full introduction to the disputation speech suggests that it
was intended to be seen as closely related to what precedes, perhaps to counterbalance the negative tone of vv.1-31 with brighter prospects, albeit including a

---

[95] HOELSCHER, *Hesekiel*, 110; COOKE, *Ezekiel*, 220; GARSCHA, *Studien*, 121.

[96] BERTHOLET, *Hesekiel*, 71, and FOHRER, *Ezechiel*, 107,114, make the division after v.32. HERNTRICH,
Ezechielprobleme, 104, and WEVERS, *Ezekiel*, 151, consider v.32 to belong neither to what precedes nor
to what follows.

[97] HERRMANN, *Ezechiel*, 125-127; ZIMMERLI, *Ezechiel*, 437-438, and EICHRODT, *Hesekiel*, 180, make the
break after v.31. EICHRODT, *Hesekiel*, 182, however, considers that the two texts belong closely
together. The quotation in v.32 illustrates the plans of the elders who came to consult Ezekiel and
gives the reason why their request was refused.

[98] BALTZER, *Ezechiel*, 2, gives no convincing justification for a division into two parts, vv.33-38 and
vv.39-44.

judgement. This lack of the full introductory formulae in no way puts in question the basic disputation speech structure, especially since similar cases occur in Ezek 11,2 and 37,11b. The phrase "what you have in mind" recalls a similar expression in Ezek 11,5, also in a disputation speech: both expressions are pejorative, as also the similar phrases with *°LH* and *lēb* in Ezek 14,4.7 and 38,10. Already in the introduction, before the words of the quotation are actually spoken, the people's quotation is being rejected: what is on their minds will not become reality.

Quotation

32   We shall be like the nations,
            like the tribes of other lands,
            serving wood and stone.

This statement is often interpreted as defiantly expressing the people's desire to be like the nations[99]. It is seen to be in the same vein as 1 Sam 8,20: "let us too be like all the nations", where the people are clamouring for a king. But in fact the tone here is similar to that found in Ezek 25,8, where Moab insults Judah by describing her as "like all the nations". The people despondently accept this as a fact. They consider they have lost their special position among the nations. Their God has abandoned them. The phrase "serving wood and stone" shows that the quotation expresses not defiance but deep despair. "Wood and stone" is a disparaging description of the gods of the nations, found in Deut 29,16; 2 Kgs 19,18 (Isa 37,19). Further texts, in Deut 4,28 and 28,36.64, list the worship of wood and stone as one of the curses to be inflicted on Israel if she fails to follow God's laws. It is precisely the realisation of such a curse that the people are now bewailing. Due to their disobedience they are condemned to the service of idols, which they describe with contempt as "wood and stone". The final phrase "serving wood and stone" is necessary to complete the sense and should not be deleted as a deuteronomic addition[100]. Such references to "wood and stone" are not exclusive to deuteronomic material and are also found elsewhere, as in Jer 2,27; 3,9 and Hab 2,19. Furthermore, when speaking of worship of wood and stone, Deuteronomy uses *°BD*, and not *ŠRT*.

The quotation expresses sentiments comparable to those found in other disputation speeches, notably in Ezek 12,27; 33,10 and 37,11b. In fact, all the

---

[99] *RSV*: "Let us be like the nations, like the tribes of the countries, and worship wood and stone." *TOB*: "Nous voulons être comme les nations, comme les clans des autres pays, servir le bois et la pierre." Eichrodt: "Wir wollen sein wie die Völker, wie die Geschlechter der (anderen) Länder." Eichrodt omits the final phrase.

[100] Eichrodt, *Hesekiel*, 181, sees the quotation as announcing the elders' plans to set up a place of sacrifice to Yahweh in Babylon, and deletes "serving wood and stone" as a result of deuteronomic editing.

quotations in disputation speeches attributed to the exiles in Ezekiel express despair and hopelessness, whereas those of the people left in Jerusalem have a confident, arrogant tone (11,3.15; 12,22; 18,2; 33,24). The overall positive tone of the refutation is a fitting reply to words expressing a loss of hope for the future. Similar encouraging replies are found in 12,28; 33,11-16 and 37,12-13. The disputation speech thus might be considered as showing in the quotation the people's despondent reaction to Ezekiel's wholly negative view of Israel's history in vv.1-31, and providing in the refutation an encouraging reply from Yahweh announcing a brighter future[101].

Programmatic Refutation

33   As I live, says the Lord Yahweh,
      with strong hand,
      and outstretched arm,
      and wrath poured out,
      I will reign over you.

The oath formula introduces the programmatic refutation, as in Ezek 18,3 and 33,11. The essence of the refutation lies in the words "I will reign over you", which are a direct rejection of the people's envisaged service of idols. V.33 is a programmatic refutation since it rejects the idea expressed by the people, while anticipating what will be explained in the coming verses. Vv.34-44 will explain just how Yahweh will assert his sovereignty over them. This is the one place in Ezekiel where Yahweh is referred to as king, whether with the verb *MLK* or the noun *melek*. A similarly unique use of *MLK* for Yahweh is found in Deutero-Isaiah, in 52,7, and in a similar context. There a herald announces that Yahweh has assumed his kingship. This proclamation is motivated by Yahweh's return to Sion (v.8). Vv. 9-10 give further reasons for jubilation: not only has Yahweh consoled and redeemed his people (v.9b), but he has bared his holy arm before the eyes of all the nations (v.10a). In Deutero-Isaiah Yahweh is thus seen as king when he takes steps to console his people and display his holiness for all the nations to see. Yahweh's assuming his kingship in the programmatic refutation in Ezek 20,33 will be explained in the succeeding verses in much the same way. Yahweh will intervene to console his people and to remedy the cry of despair voiced in v.32. But at the same time he will demonstrate his power before the eyes of the nations. The three sections of the refutation (vv.34-38.39-42.43-44), and the central section in particular, will make this second point clear: the scattered people are to be gathered together from among the nations (v.34); Yahweh will display his holiness through the people

---

[101] ZIMMERLI, *Ezechiel*, 453.

before the eyes of the nations (v.41); he will take action for the sake of his name (v.44), so that he will not be despised by the nations. Thus Yahweh's taking up his reign is, as in Isa 52,7-10, not only an answer to the people's despair, but also a demonstration of his holiness before the nations. *MLK* in v.33 needs explanation, and is fully explained in the three sections of the refutation.

The programmatic refutation uses three phrases to accompany the verb. The phrases "with strong hand" and "with outstretched arm", whether used separately or together, almost always refer to Yahweh's activity in the exodus[102]. The use of these phrases suggests Yahweh is planning another intervention on the same grand scale. The final phrase "with wrath poured out" is only found here, though the phrase *ŠPK ḥēmâ* is commonly used of Yahweh in Ezekiel, notably in 20,8.13.21. The presence of the final phrase could well be an allusion to the purifying judgement in vv.34-38. The three phrases will return in v.34, in the first section of the refutation.

Refutation (in three parts)

I

34   I will bring you out from the peoples,
            I will gather you from the lands
            where you were scattered,
            with strong hand,
            and outstretched arm,
            and wrath poured out.

35   I will bring you to the desert of the peoples,
            and I will enter into judgement with you there,
            face to face.

36   Just as I judged your fathers
            in the desert of the land of Egypt,
            so will I judge you, says the Lord Yahweh.

37   I will make you pass under the staff,
            and I will bring you under the bond of
            the covenant.

---

[102] Both expressions are used in Deut 4,34; 5,15; 26,8; Jer 32,21; Ps 136,12. "With strong hand" is found in Exod 13,9; 32,11; Deut 6,21; 7,8; 9,26; Dan 9,15. "With outstretched arm" appears in Exod 6,6; 2 Kgs 17,36. The former phrase is employed in Exod 3,19 and 6,1 in the context of Pharaoh's role in the exodus, and in Num 20,20 in a reference to Edom.

38   I will purge out from among you
          the rebels and those who rose up against me.
          From the land where they were staying
          I will bring them out,
          but they will not reach the land of Israel.
          And you will know that I am Yahweh.

> In v.38 *yābô'* is to be read *yābō'û*
> (haplography).

II

39   And you, house of Israel, thus says the Lord Yahweh:
          each one of you, cast away your idols,
          and you will no longer defile my holy name
          with your gifts and your idols.
40   For on my holy mountain,
          on the high mountain of Israel,
          says the Lord Yahweh,
          there all the house of Israel,
          all of it in the land, will serve me,
          there I will accept them,
          there I will require your contributions
          and the first of your gifts
          with all your holy offerings.
41   As a pleasing odour I will accept you,
          when I bring you out from the peoples,
          and gather you from the lands
          where you were scattered,
          and display my holiness through you
          before the eyes of the nations.
42   And you will know that I am Yahweh,
          when I bring you to the land of Israel,
          to the land I swore to give to your fathers.

> In v.39 read *hašlîkû* for *l^ekû* as in v.7,
> and delete the rest of v.39a as a gloss.

III

43   And you will remember there
          your ways and all your deeds
          by which you defiled yourselves,

and you will loathe yourselves
for all the wicked deeds you committed.

44   And you will know that I am Yahweh
when I act towards you for the sake of my name,
not according to your evil ways
and your corrupt deeds,
house of Israel, says the Lord Yahweh.

The refutation in three stages, vv.34-38.39-42.43-44, not only illustrates how Yahweh proposes to take up his kingship, saving his people and demonstrating his holiness before the nations, but also and above all rejects the people's resignation to serving idols. They will not be reduced to serving wood and stone, for Yahweh has not abandoned them. Indeed, they must be purified by his judgement and reject all idolatrous practices, so that they may be worthy to come to worship and present gifts on his holy mountain. The first section, vv.34-38, announces a judgement which is to purge out those who rebel against Yahweh. This judgement is a preparation for the service of Yahweh announced in the second section. The judgement in vv.34-38 does not alter the basic tenor of the refutation, which is one of promise. The presence of a judgement here should not therefore lead to the conclusion that the quotation contained words of arrogance to be punished rather than words of despair answered by a promise. The judgement is merely the first stage. The second section begins with a plea by Yahweh to cast away idols. In the third section the people look back on their past actions and rue their evil deeds. Each section thus rejects explicitly or implicitly the service of idols which the people see as their future.

The use of the word *šām* ties the three sections of the refutation together. In the central section it occurs three times in v.40. It is there, on the holy mountain of Yahweh, that the people will offer worship to Yahweh; any idea of worshipping elsewhere, and thus of serving other gods, is categorically rejected by this threefold use of *šām* at the heart of the refutation. But *šām* is also found in the other two sections: in v.35 it refers to the place of the purifying judgement which is to purge out those unworthy to offer worship on Yahweh's holy mountain; and in v.43 *šām* refers again to the land of Israel where the people will look back with horror at their evil deeds. Yahweh will take them back "there", so that they will have no doubt that he, Yahweh, is the God they must worship, and he the one they must serve. The concentric use of *šām* can be seen as further concentrating the attention on the heart of the refutation in v.40: the people will not worship idols, for it is their calling to serve Yahweh there on his holy mountain.

In the first section of the refutation Yahweh declares that he will gather together those scattered in various lands for a judgement in the "desert of the peoples". The expression seems not to refer to a specific location, but to be a symbolic antitype to the desert of Egypt (v.36)[103]. As a shepherd Yahweh makes his people pass under the staff to count them[104]. The reference to the "bond of the covenant" in v.37, though unparalleled, fits suitably in the context of a coming judgement which will purge out those who have disregarded the laws of that covenant, leaving a people who can worthily offer worship to Yahweh[105].

V.39, the first verse of the second section of the refutation, presents problems. Several attempts have been made to preserve v.39a, but these involve having Yahweh invite those who will to continue in the service of idols. This seems quite out of keeping with the purpose of the refutation, which is to declare that the people will not worship wood and stone, but will return to Israel to worship Yahweh on his holy mountain. It does not seem possible to maintain the text as it stands even by considering Yahweh's invitation to serve idols as a rhetorical ploy intended to provoke a change of heart in those who still cling to idols[106]. Yahweh in fact calls for a rejection of idol worshipping. His call is preceded by the messenger formula, which gives it further weight. The people will bring their offerings and worship Yahweh on his holy mountain. Here lies the heart of the refutation of the serving of wood and stone which the people envisaged. The triple $šām$ stresses that it is there in Israel that they will offer worship[107]. This is the one reference in Ezekiel to "my holy mountain", and is followed swiftly by Ezekiel's expression "the high mountain of Israel", found again in 17,23. Vv. 39-41 emphasise the holiness of Yahweh: his holy name will no longer be defiled; they will present holy offerings on his holy mountain; he will show his holiness through them before the eyes of the nations. They will know that he is Yahweh, a holy God, who has chosen a people to serve him and does not allow this people to be like the nations in serving wood and stone.

---

[103] ZIMMERLI, *Ezechiel*, 455-456.

[104] The expression ʿBR taḥat haśśābet in v.37 is employed also in Lev 27,32. A similar expression is seen in Jer 33,13. Only in Ezek 20,37, however, is Yahweh the subject and the verb hiphil.

[105] BERTHOLET, *Hesekiel*, 73; FOHRER, *Ezechiel*, 115; ZIMMERLI, *Ezechiel*, 437, and WEVERS, *Ezekiel*, 159, propose to follow the LXX, reading $b^e mispār$ and omitting $habb^e rit$ as dittography. The resulting expression would be a close parallel to v.37a and similar to 1 Chr 9,28. The MT, however, seems to offer a richer text.

[106] The majority of translations and commentaries have Yahweh invite the people to serve idols. *RSV*: "As for you, O house of Israel, thus says the Lord God: Go serve every one of you his idols, now and hereafter, if you will not listen to me." *TOB*: "Quant à vous, maison d'Israël, ainsi parle le Seigneur Dieu: Que chacun aille servir ses idoles; mais ensuite on verra bien si vous ne m'écoutez pas." COOKE, *Ezekiel*, 222, preserves the text but admits that "a blank is left to be filled by the imagination". EICHRODT, *Hesekiel*, 168, maintains the text with the exception of w^eʾaḥar, which he considers a relic of an alternative reading. WEVERS, *Ezekiel*, 159-160, proposes that w^eʾaḥar could be a corruption of a marginal w'ḥrh "and I shall be angered". Of those who change the consonantal text more radically BERTHOLET, *Hesekiel*, 73, proposes to read baʿārû for ʿābōdû and to omit l^ekû. Similarly, FOHRER, *Ezechiel*, 115, who also proposes ʾabb^e dû. The confused state of the text advises following ZIMMERLI, *Ezechiel*, 437, in reading haślîkû as in 20,7 for l^ekû and disregarding the remaining words of v.39a.

[107] The temporary change to the third person in v.40 with bêt yiśrāʾēl as subject does not necessitate any text critical operation. Thus ZIMMERLI, *Ezechiel*, 457.

The final stage of the refutation concerns the people's recognition of their own wickedness and stresses that Yahweh has acted with them not according to these deeds but for the sake of his name, in order to demonstrate his holiness before the nations. The same sequence of remembering, loathing and knowing is found in Ezek 36,31-32, again at the conclusion of an announcement of Yahweh's future deeds in favour of his people, deeds performed for the sake of his name. Israel is not to be like the nations, serving wood and stone, but to be the instrument whereby Yahweh displays his holiness before them, when he brings his people back to worship him in the land.

Conclusion

The disputation speech in Ezek 20,32-44 thus looks to the future and gives a hopeful prospect to contrast with Ezekiel's portrayal of Israel's dismal past. The three sections of the refutation serve as a counterbalance to the three stages of Israel's history portrayed in vv.1-31. The recurrence in vv.42.44 of the phrases "raise my hand" and "act for the sake of my name", prominent in vv.1-31, serves to strengthen the link between the two units. Yahweh will continue his actions in favour of his people in spite of their evil deeds and for the sake of his name. He will purify them and bring them to serve him. He will not abandon them to the service of other gods.

Ezekiel 33,10-20

Context, Structure and Unity

Ezek 33,10-20 has a structure similar to Ezek 18,1-20, that of the extended disputation speech, with the exception that the rejoinder is given twice and twice receives a reply.

One formula of the coming of the word introduces the whole of 33,1-20. In vv.1-9 Ezekiel is compared to a watchman in his activity of instructing his people to repent. Vv.10-20 show one way in which this activity is performed in the specific context of a reply to the people's quotation in v.10, which laments their incapacity to change their fate. The address "son of man" and renewed command to speak in v.12 should on the grounds of the content not be considered as beginning a new unit, although they do do so in v.10[108]. Vv.12-16 in fact provide the refutation, explaining the programmatic refutation in v.11. The refutation is in two sections, dealing with perversion from good to evil and conversion from evil to good. The two rejoinders and replies follow in vv.17-20. Vv. 10-20 are

---

[108] FOHRER, *Ezechiel*, 182, by contrast, considers vv.10-11 to have been added to vv.12-20 as part of the gradual building up of Ezek 33.

bound together by the theme *ŠWB* which, except for one instance in v.18, where it denotes perversion, refers to conversion from evil to good. *ŠWB* also binds this disputation speech to vv.1-9 where, although the root *ŠWB* does not appear until v.9, the theme is the prophet's responsibility for the people's conversion.

The root *ḤYH* is introduced by the quotation and dominates the refutation (vv.11.(12).13.15.16.19), another sign that vv.10-20 are a unit. To the people's cry "How are we to live?" a practical answer is given.

Thus Ezek 33,10-20 shows a unity of content and the extended disputation speech structure found in 18,1-20[109].

Introduction and Quotation

10   And you, son of man,
        speak to the house of Israel:
        You say this:
        Yes, our transgressions and our sins
        are upon us,
        due to them we are wasting away,
        how are we to live?

The exiles here show they are aware that it is their own sins which have brought disaster upon them. Rather than the arrogant spirit betrayed in Ezek 18,2, it is a cloud of despair which hangs over them. Their own sins have led to disaster.

Niphal *MQQ* is found in similar contexts in Ezek 4,17; 24,23 and Lev 26,39. In lively figurative language it expresses both the people's awareness of the effects of their sins, and their despair at being able to do nothing to avoid these effects.

The suffixes *-ênû* and *-ānû* are frequently found in words of lament. In the despairing words of Ezek 37,11b these suffixes will again be seen in the quotation of a disputation speech. Isa 59,12 presents an abundance of such sounds with similar vocabulary to Ezek 33,10.

---

[109] DEL OLMO LETE, "Ez. 33,1-20", 30-31, rightly defends the original unity of both 18,1-20 and 33,10-20. AUVRAY, "Guetteur", 200-203, also defends the original unity of 18,1-20, but in 33,10-20 considers vv.12-13, which deal with perversion rather than conversion, to have been added at a time of particular danger of apostasy. It is better to explain their presence by reference to Ezekiel's casuistic style: both possibilities of *ŠWB* are presented, though conversion is obviously the principal point. Auvray gives no reason for his contention that vv.17-20 are later additions.

Programmatic Refutation

11   Say to them:
          As I live, says the Lord Yahweh,
          I do not desire the death of the wicked man,
          but rather that a wicked man turn from his way
          that he might live.
          Turn back, turn back from your evil ways,
          for why should you die, house of Israel?

     The command to speak is repeated (three times in vv.10.11.12) and the oath
formula introduces the programmatic refutation, as in Ezek 18,3 and 20,33.
V.11 is to be considered a programmatic refutation for it gives a concise reply
to the quotation and prepares for the explanation in vv.12-16. V.11a is parallel
to 18,23. Comparison of its two positions within the respective texts indicates
that its position in 33,10-20 is the original, since in 18,21-32 it interrupts the
presentation of the two cases, the conversion of the wicked man and the perversion of the virtuous man[110]. V.11b, the explicit call to conversion, is much
amplified in 18,30b-32.

Refutation

12   And you, son of man,
          say to the sons of your people:
          the justice of the just man
          will not save him when he sins,
          and the wickedness of the wicked man
          will not be an obstacle to him
          when he turns from his evil.
13   When I say about the just man:
          he shall certainly live,
          and he trusts in his righteousness and does evil,
          all his acts of righteousness
          will not be remembered,
          and he will die due to the evil he has committed.
14   And when I say to the wicked man:
          you will certainly die,
          and he turns from his sin,
          and acts justly and righteously,

---

[110] ZIMMERLI, *Ezechiel*, 413, finds 18,23 to be quite unexpected and stylistically awkward.

15   the wicked man returns the pledge,
he pays back what he has robbed,
he walks in the commands of life
in order to do no evil,
he shall certainly live,
he shall not die.

16   All the sins he committed will not be
held against him,
he has acted justly and righteously,
he shall certainly live.

> V.12b is to be considered a gloss, since
> it disturbs the parallelism of v.12a and
> lays too much stress on the perversion
> of the just man. *bāh* in v.12b also has
> no antecedent.
> In v.13b read *ṣidqōtāyw* with the Qere.
> In v.16 read *ḥaṭṭō'tāyw* with the Qere.

As in Ezek 18,1-20, the programmatic refutation here is followed by the presentation of the cases, on this occasion the two possibilities of perversion and conversion, which are set down schematically in v.12a.

The verb *NṢL* (v.12) is omitted in the corresponding material in 18,21-32 and is found only here with righteousness as the subject. It is however commonly used of saving life in Ezekiel, notably in 33,9 of the prophet saving his own life and in 14,20 of Noah, Danel and Job saving their lives "due to their righteousness". *KŠL* (v.12) is also absent from 18,21-32, though 18,30 uses the phrase *mikšôl ᶜāwōn* common in Ezekiel. V.12a has in fact no close counterpart in 18,21-32, which launches straight into the case of the conversion of the wicked in v.21 with no trace of an introduction.

The case of the perversion of the just man is dealt with first in v.13. He is not even directly addressed by Yahweh; the third person is used. The second case, which is the real issue at stake, will be developed at greater length. V.15 digresses to show how the newly converted wicked man shows his repentance by putting right to some extent the evil he has perpetrated: pledges are returned, stolen goods restored[111]. This stressing of the second case, the conversion of the wicked man, is not found in the parallel material in 18,21-22.24, where the sequence of cases is reversed and both cases are referred to in the third person. The stress here is entirely in keeping with the context. The lamenting exiles can change their future by returning from their sins to a life of justice and righteousness.

---

[111] *rāšāᶜ* can be maintained in spite of the objections of ZIMMERLI, *Ezechiel*, 797, and EICHRODT, *Hesekiel*, 314. It emphasises the wicked man's conversion.

Rejoinders and Replies

17   The sons of your people will say:
          The way of the Lord cannot be fathomed.
          But it is their way which cannot be fathomed.
18   When a just man turns from his righteousness and does evil,
          he will die because of it.
19   And when a wicked man turns from his wickedness
          and acts justly and righteously,
          he will live because of it.
20   You will say:
          The way of the Lord cannot be fathomed.
          I will judge each one of you
          according to his deeds, house of Israel.

The rejoinder and reply, already seen in 18,19-20, are found here too. On this occasion the same rejoinder is made twice (vv.17a.20a) and twice a reply is given. These words of the people are usually rendered: "The way of the Lord is not just", to which it is replied that it is the people's way which is "not just"[112]. Such an interpretation fits with great difficulty into the context. The people are lamenting that death is their lot (v.10), they are offered a chance of life in the refutation. Is it logical that they should immediately object, accusing Yahweh of injustice[113]?

The verb *TKN*, which in the piel clearly means "measure", as demonstrated by Job 28,25 and Isa 40,12, in the qal is used of Yahweh's ability to penetrate or weigh up the hearts of men in the only three MT uses, Prov 16,2; 21,2 and 24,12[114]. The one niphal use of *TKN* outside Ezek 33,17.20 (and 18,25.29) is 1 Sam 2,3b *welō' nitkenû 'ālilôt*. This is often taken as a reference to man's evil deeds, and with the assistance of the qere reading *welô* referred to Yahweh the sense becomes "by him actions are weighed"[115]. Others, following the LXX, read *'ēl tōkēn* and render as a reference to God's acts: "a god who balances his actions"[116]. It would seem, however, that the text as it stands is a close parallel

---

[112] Thus the *RSV*. *TOB*: "Le chemin du Seigneur n'est pas équitable." ZIMMERLI: "Der Weg Jahwes ist nicht richtig."

[113] ZIMMERLI, *Ezechiel*, 807, considers vv.17-20 an addition due to the apparent clash of the rejoinder with the quotation in v.10. One might also wonder whether the prophet would have used such an expression if he wished to question the justice of Yahweh's ways. Prov 21,2a simply uses *yāšār* in reference to the apparent justice of man's ways.

[114] McKANE, *Proverbs*, 235, renders *TKN* in Prov 16,2 "weigh up". He is critical (p. 496) of the translation "weigh", which is proposed by SCOTT, *Proverbs*, 104, 106, due to a supposed link with Egyptian mythology.

[115] Thus *RSV*. *TOB*: "c'est lui qui pèse les actions". HERTZBERG, *Samuelbücher*, 18, renders "und von ihm werden Taten gewogen". TOURNAY, "Cantique d'Anne", 554, 560, renders in similar fashion.

[116] Thus recently McCARTER, *I Samuel*, 67, 69. BOER, "Einige Bemerkungen", 54, suggests a similar rendering as an alternative. DAHOOD, *Psalms*, II, 211, proposes the translation "And the Victor is the

to Ezek 33,17.20. *lō'* with the verb *TKN* in the niphal precedes "acts" or "ways" as the subject. When referred to man's evil acts and with the habitual translation of niphal *TKN* as "be in order" or "be right", the rendering becomes "men's acts are not in order"[117]. But *ʿălilôt* can be taken, as in Ps 9,12; 77,13; 78,11; 103,7 and 105,1, as a reference to God's acts, and niphal *TKN* is better interpreted "to be weighed up" or "to be fathomed" in conformity with the qal uses in Proverbs. In this way 1 Sâm 2,3b should be rendered "his (Yahweh's) deeds cannot be fathomed", which provides a most satisfactory parallel to the preceding "for Yahweh is a god of great knowledge". God's deeds are beyond human judgement. This one other use of niphal *TKN* thus sheds unexpected light on Ezek 33,17.20, which should not be rendered "the way of the Lord is not just", but rather "the way of the Lord cannot be fathomed". 1 Sam 2,3b and Ezek 33,17.20 are close parallels both in syntax and in sense.

Thus the people are not impugning God's justice, which would be quite out of keeping with the context, but rather expressing their surprise and their difficulty in understanding Yahweh's ways. The ways of Yahweh cannot be fathomed by them, for they had thought to waste away till death due to their sins. Now it is announced that through conversion their sins can be forgotten as if they were never committed. One senses also that the rejoinder "the way of the Lord cannot be fathomed" contains an element of reluctance on the part of the people to change their lives. This interpretation of *TKN* shows the unity of the disputation speech, and that the rejoinder follows smoothly after the refutation, as happened in 18,19.

Yahweh takes up their rejoinder in his reply in v.17b that it is rather their ways which cannot be understood. The interpretation of *TKN* proposed here is again apt. Yahweh is amazed that, knowing the way to life, the people do not follow it; their ways too are beyond comprehension! There follows, in vv.18-19, a summary of what was explained in the refutation. The rejoinder of the people is repeated in v.20, this time provoking the stark reply: "I will judge each one of you according to his deeds." The issue should already be clear to them: it is now up to them.

In 18,25-32 the same rejoinder is again found twice. The replies are however given at greater length and vv.30b-32 develop the call to conversion found in its original position in 33,11, with the notable addition of new material in v.31a.

---

weigher of actions" without tampering with the consonantal text. In "Parallel Pairs", 70, Dahood modifies this translation slightly, rendering "and by the Omnipotent actions are weighed".

[117] Thus STOEBE, *Das erste Buch Samuelis*, 100, 101, renders "und schändliche Taten bestehen nicht" or "haben keinen Bestand". Similarly, BOER, "Einige Bemerkungen", 53.

Conclusion

From this analysis the unity of Ezek 33,10-20 is evident. The people's lament is answered by the prophet's reply that new life is possible through conversion. The people express their incredulity that life is really possible for
them, but Yahweh assures them and insists that the way to life is open provided
they reject their wickedness.

Ezekiel 33,23-29

Context, Structure and Unity

One formula of the coming of the word introduces Ezek 33,23-33. Vv.23-29
are a disputation speech with two refutations, marked by introductory formulae in v.25 and v.27. Ezek 33,30-33 begins with a quotation of the people's
words, but this quotation is an illustration of the exiles' attitude to Ezekiel's
preaching, and is not given with a view to being refuted. This latter unit cannot
therefore be considered a disputation speech[118]. The two units are placed
together as evidence of the attitudes found after 587 both back in the land and
in Babylon.

The quotation in v.24 is challenged by two refutations. The first in vv.25-26
challenges the quotation directly by taking up the claim to possession of the
land; after the introductory command to speak it is addressed in the second
person to those who uttered the quotation. The second refutation by contrast
refers to these same people in Israel in the third person. Thus a similar process
is seen to that found in Ezek 11,16.17. The first refutation is given as if addressed directly to the speakers of the quotation, while the second is directed to the
real audience, the exiles, and thus refers to those in Israel in the third person.
The difference between the refutations in these two similar disputation
speeches is that whereas the refutations in 11,16.17 spoke of the exiles, those in
33,25-26.27-29 consider the fate of those left behind in Israel. Of the two refutations here the first refutation has more weight, since it is there that the claim
to the land is explicitly challenged[119].

Introduction

23   And the word of Yahweh came to me saying:

---

[118] ZIMMERLI, *Ezechiel*, 55*, describes the quotation in 33,30 as purely illustrative.
[119] ZIMMERLI, *Ezechiel*, 817-818, by contrast, while regarding the whole unit as a disputation
speech, considers vv.25-26 as preparing for vv.27-29, which contain the real message, introduced by an
oath.

24   Son of man, the inhabitants of these ruins
        in the land of Israel are saying:

The description of the speakers as living among the ruins indicates that the
coming quotation is attributed to those still remaining in Jerusalem after its
destruction. The saying appears to belong to a period some time after the
actual destruction of the city[120].

Quotation

24   One was Abraham, and he inherited the land;
        we are many, so the land is our inheritance.

The quotation takes the form of two parallel statements, each consisting of
two clauses. A double chiastic link binds the statements together. The words
make a similar claim to that found in Ezek 11,15. But the reason given here is
not that the exiles have gone far from Yahweh. Those who have survived two
deportations regard themselves as God's chosen ones. God's favour has decreed
the land should belong to them. As in 11,15, the niphal of *NTN* implies it is God
who has bequeathed them the land. They give the reason for their claim by
referring to the faith of their fathers. Abraham was alone when the land was
promised to him as his property. A numerous posterity was also assured him[121].
The promise to Abraham of a numerous posterity has been fulfilled in them and
they can thus expect the other major promise of the possession of the land to be
realised for them too. It is noteworthy that Isa 51,2 also calls attention to the
fact that Abraham was alone, in order to encourage and console the people by
consideration of the blessings showered on him in his need by Yahweh. The
speakers of the quotation in Ezek 33,24 consider such blessings to be their
right, because they are Abraham's descendants[122]. Thus they use Abraham to
assert their claim to possession of the land and to encourage themselves that
God's blessings will continue to be forthcoming[123].

---

[120] It would seem therefore ill-advised to propose that the fugitive of vv.21-22 informed Ezekiel of
the saying, as FOHRER, *Ezechiel*, 188, suggests.

[121] References to Abraham inheriting the land are to be found in Gen 15,7-8; 28,4; Exod 6,8; Deut
1,8; 9,5. Exod 6,8 also employs the term *môrāšâ*. Promises to Abraham of a numerous posterity are announced in Gen 16,10; 17,2; 22,17.

[122] The same reliance on being the seed of Abraham reappears in the NT: Matt 3,9; Luke 3,8; John
8,33.39.

[123] EICHRODT, *Hesekiel*, 320, regards the claim to the land as secondary and considers the primary
aim of the quotation to be to encourage reconstruction. The refutations show that at least for the
exiles, to whom the speech was addressed, the major issue here is the inheritance of the land.

The Refutations

In Ezek 11,7-10.11-12 and 11,16.17 a chronological sequence was noted between the two refutations in each disputation speech. The first dealt with the
contemporary situation while the second looked to the future. In 33,25-26.27-29
too a chronological sequence may be seen. Vv.25-26 deal with the past and present transgressions which render the claim to the land unacceptable. Vv.27-29
look to the future punishment due for these sins.

First Refutation

25   So, say to them: thus says the Lord Yahweh:
         You eat with the blood,
         you raise your eyes to your idols,
         you shed blood,
         and are you to inherit the land?
26   You have relied on your swords,
         you have committed abominations,
         you have each defiled the wife of his neighbour,
         and are you to inherit the land?

         In v.25 ʿēnēkem is to be read ʿênêkem.

The first refutation tackles the claim directly. Evil conduct invalidates the
claim to the land. After the introductory formulae Yahweh describes the conduct of those left in the land. Two groups of three actions are each followed by
the rhetorical question "and are you to inherit the land?" The whole of this first
refutation is addressed directly to the speakers of the quotation, those still sur-
viving in Israel, as if they were actually present.

Eating meat with the blood is forbidden in various legal texts, particularly
in Leviticus and Deuteronomy, though the expression 'KL ʿal-haddām is found
only in Lev 19,26 and in the narrative text 1 Sam 14,32-34[124]. The phrase "raise
one's eyes to idols" is found in the longer lists of transgressions in Ezek
18,6.12.15. "Shedding of blood" is frequent in Ezekiel and found again in Ezek
18,10[125]. These first three actions are given in the yiqtol, and are rounded off by

---

[124] Further legal texts: Gen 9,4; Lev 3,17; 7,26-27; 17,10.12.14; Deut 12,16.23; 15,23. Cooke, Ezekiel,
368, and Fohrer, Ezechiel, 187, propose the reading "on the mountains" as in 18,6.11.15 and 22,9. Zimmerli, Ezechiel, 820, however, contends that reference to worship on the high places would be obsolete
by this time and that a reference to the law regarding eating with the blood would be more likely here.

[125] The classic formulation forbidding the shedding of blood is in Gen 9,6. Ezek 22,3.4.6.9.12 refer
to the "blood-stained city". Ezek 16,38 and 23,45 concern the judgement on those who shed blood.
Other occurrences in Ezek 22,27 and 36,18.

the rhetorical question which directly ridicules the claim to possession of the land[126].

The second group of three crimes is formulated in the qatal. The reference to "relying on the sword" is unique here in the MT[127]. By contrast, the phrase *ʿŚH tôʿēbâ* is most common. The designation "abomination" is used for a wide range of transgressions in all parts of the OT, often sins due to foreign influence, and especially in Leviticus, Deuteronomy and Proverbs[128]. In Ezekiel it is often used as a euphemism, as here and 18,12, where it is not apparent what specific crime is intended. In v.29 the word will reappear in the plural to embrace all manner of crime, as in 18,13[129]. The final sin listed is adultery, expressed as a crime of defiling the wife of another, as in 18,6.11.15. Once again, the group of three misdemeanours is concluded by the rhetorical question "and are you to inherit the land?"

Second Refutation

27   Thus you will say to them:
         thus says the Lord Yahweh:
         As I live,
         those who are in the ruins
         will fall by the sword,
         he who is in the open field,
         I will give him to the beasts to devour him,
         those in strongholds and caves
         will die by the plague.

28   And I will make the land desolate and devastated,
         and the pride of its strength will be destroyed,
         and the mountains of Israel will be desolate
         with no man crossing them.

29   And they will know that I am Yahweh,
         when I make the land desolate and devastated
         for all the abominations they have committed.

The introduction to the second refutation includes the oath formula, found also in Ezek 18,3; 20,33 and 33,11 in programmatic refutations. This second

---

[126] REVENTLOW, *Wächter*, 101, refers to similar questions following the indication of transgressions in Ezek 14,3 and 20,31.

[127] ZIMMERLI, *Ezechiel*, 820, suggests it is an eloquent comment on the lawlessness of the times.

[128] GERSTENBERGER, "*tʿb* pi.", 1051-1055.

[129] *ʿăśîten* can be maintained as facilitating pronunciation before the following tau. See COOKE, *Ezekiel*, 371; ZIMMERLI, *Ezechiel*, 816, and GKC 44 k. In any case, *TOB* seems to give too much weight to the humble nun when it renders: "vous, les femmes, vous commettez ce qui est abominable".

refutation announces punishment for the continuing evil actions of those left in Israel. In v.27 the people in the land are distributed in three locations and threatened with three corresponding punishments. Jeremiah often refers to the sword, hunger and the plague as agents of punishment, as in Jer 24,10 and 29,18. Ezekiel sometimes introduces wild beasts as a fourth scourge, as in Ezek 5,17 and 14,12-20. In this disputation speech the scourge of hunger is replaced by wild beasts, perhaps due to the situation after 587, when hunger due to siege was no longer a threat. Alliteration in $b^e h\breve{o}r\bar{a}b\hat{o}t\ bah.ereb$ consigns those in the ruins to the sword. Those in the open country are to be the prey of wild beasts, though elsewhere (Ezek 7,15; 26,6.8) this location is the scene of death by the sword. Finally, those in hiding in inaccessible strongholds and caves death will seek out by the plague.

In v.28 Yahweh announces the total devastation of the land using language often employed for such announcements. The alliterative phrase $\check{s}^e m\bar{a}m\hat{a}$ $\hat{u}m^e\check{s}amm\hat{a}$, threatened against Israel also in Ezek 6,14, is directed to Edom in Ezek 35,3.(7). The destruction of the "pride of their strength" was predicted in Ezek 7,24 and 24,21, when Yahweh announced the coming defilement of the temple. Now that that source of pride has been destroyed, he threatens the complete devastation of the land, their only remaining source of pride. A similar threat was made against the land of Egypt in Ezek 30,6.18. The mountains of Israel, first menaced in Ezek 6,2, will be desolate, for no human being will cross them. Similar references to the lack of human activity in a ravaged land are seen in Ezek 14,15 and Jer 9,9.11[130]. V.29 closes the refutation with an extended formula of recognition of Yahweh, which reiterates the reason for the coming devastation.

Conclusion

This disputation speech gives a further negative answer to the claims of those in the land, claims first heard in Ezek 11,15. Their claim seems more justified now, for they have survived the deportations and even the destruction of the city. But, however favoured they may seem, they will nevertheless have no part in the future of Israel, for they have shown utter disregard for Yahweh's laws. They are destined to be swept away before the return of those in exile, the true inheritors of the land.

---

[130] WEVERS, *Ezekiel*, 254, considers this promise of further destruction in vv.28-29 to be out of place after 587. He suggests vv.25-29 were the original reply to 11,15 and that v.24 is a creation of an editor. But, as ZIMMERLI, *Ezechiel*, 820, has pointed out, Jer 52,30 indicates continued devastation of the land. And quite apart from the actual situation, Ezekiel is using strong stereotyped language of destruction in order to condemn the claims made in v.24.

Ezekiel 37,11b-13

Context, Structure and Unity

The major problem raised by Ezek 37,1-14 is the exact nature of the relationship of vv.11-14 to vv.1-10, and the precise role of v.11. The section seems to present a vision followed by its explanation, which contains a disputation
speech[131]. Close examination, however, reveals that the actual disputation
speech structure begins with the introduction and the quotation in v.11b. V.11a
belongs to the vision. After the prophet had been brought to the scene of the
vision (vv.1-2), the words addressed to him by Yahweh began in v.3 with the address "son of man" and the question "can these bones live?" Again at the end of
the vision narrative in v.11a Ezekiel is addressed as "son of man", and then told
in a brief sentence the whole meaning of the vision: "these bones — they are the
whole house of Israel". The address to the prophet as "son of man" thus forms
the framework of Yahweh's words to the prophet within the vision. The vision
needs the explanation provided in v.11a, and a separate unit begins in v.11b
where the disputation speech structure becomes apparent[132].

The text of v.11a, the explanation of the vision, is readily understood as it
stands. The final *hēmmâ*, masculine in spite of the feminine *ʿaṣāmôt* due to the
sense, is similar to other cases where the demonstrative pronoun recapitulates
the subject, as in Gen 41,25-27; Exod 3,5; Num 13,32 and Qoh 5,18[133]. Just as
Joseph interprets Pharaoh's dream in Gen 41,25-27, so here Yahweh interprets
the vision given to the prophet: "these bones — they are the whole house of
Israel". The explanation of the vision is thus strikingly brief. In this regard it
might be compared to the explanation of Nathan's parable in 2 Sam 12,7a,
where the statement "you are the man!" provides a devastating conclusion[134].
Similarly, in Ezek 37,11a brevity of explanation makes the message of the
vision all the more powerful. Thus the disputation speech begins in v.11b with
an impersonal "they are saying" introduced by *hinnēh*[135].

---

[131] ZIMMERLI, *Ezechiel*, 888, considers vv.11-14 to be the explanation of the image in vv.1-10. This
explanation is in the form of a disputation speech. On the other hand, BALTZER, *Ezechiel*, 114, regards
vv.1-10 as the original vision, separate from what follows and needing no explanation. HOEFFKEN,
"Beobachtungen", 305, takes vv.1-10 as a unit which contains certain additions.

[132] HOSSFELD, *Untersuchungen*, 363, correctly sees that the major break lies between v.11a and
v.11b, and that the disputation speech begins at v.11b.

[133] Other examples are given in GKC 141 h.

[134] HERTZBERG, *Samuelbücher*, 258, and STOLZ, *Samuel*, 241, suggest that v.7a originally was the
end of Nathan's speech.

[135] Various changes have been proposed for *hēmmâ hinnēh*. BERTHOLET, *Hesekiel*, 126, and FOHRER,
Ezechiel, 209, propose *hēnnâ wᵉhinnām*. BALTZER, *Ezechiel*, 101-102, takes *hēmmâ* with v.11b, even
though he finds it clumsy. HOSSFELD, *Untersuchungen*, 361-362, does the same, and likewise considers
the resulting order in the second half of v.11 as irregular. He is however held back from taking
hēmmâ with v.11a by the fact that such a use of the demonstrative pronoun is found nowhere else in

   The division of the text into two units is further confirmed by the difference in the image found in vv.1-11a and in vv.12-13. The tension between the
vision of bones lying on a battlefield, and the idea of resuscitation from graves
might not of itself lead to a division of the text[136]. The principal reasons for
division into two units arise from form and structure. But the change in the
metaphor which becomes apparent in v.12, where people are to be raised up
from tombs, not from dry bones lying on a plain, adds further weight to the
view that it is correct to see two units here. The phrase in the quotation, "our
bones are dried up", which on grounds of vocabulary might seem to be closely
tied to vv.1-11a, is rather to be considered part of the lament of the people who
consider themselves condemned to waste away until death and the tomb. The
sentiments are of utter despair and hopelessness, like those expressed in the
quotation in Ezek 33,10. It seems probable that the reference to dry bones in
the quotation of the disputation speech led to its being placed here immediately
after the conclusion of Ezekiel's famous vision.
   V.11b thus provides the quotation which is refuted in vv.12-13, concluding
with an extended formula of recognition of Yahweh. V.14, however, does not
seem to belong to the original refutation. Though "my spirit" might seem to
arise from Ezek 36,26-28, it is bestowed here "so that you might live". The verse
thus takes up again part of 37,6a. This, along with the second formula of
recognition of Yahweh in two verses, suggests that v.14 was added here to bind
the disputation speech more closely to the vision[137].

Introduction and Quotation

11b   They are saying:
        Our bones are dried up,
        and our hope has perished,
        we have been cut off.

   The brevity of the introduction can well be explained by the disputation
speech's having been attached later to the vision.
   The words of the quotation are an expression of despair similar to that
found in Ezek 33,10. The suffixes -ênû and -ānû reappear and three phrases add
weight to the lament.
   The phrase "our bones are dried up" brings together two elements found

---

Ezekiel. However, the use is correct and understandable here, since Ezekiel had to affirm with some
conviction that those bones were the whole house of Israel.
   [136] Thus emphatically ZIMMERLI, *Ezechiel*, 888.
   [137] BALTZER, *Ezechiel*, 107, defends a similar position. ZIMMERLI, *Ezechiel*, 889, sees the plethora of
forms here as a sign of a solemn conclusion.

elsewhere in words of lament. Ps 22,15 gives the seemingly literal "and all my bones are disjointed". Ps 102,4 laments "and my bones burn". But Ps 31,11 "and my bones waste away (ʿŠŠ)" is closest to the lament here. YBŠ is used similarly to express lack of hope in Ps 22,16 and 102,5.12, as also in Num 11,6.

The second phrase states without metaphors the essence of the complaint, "our hope has perished". Similar words were used of the lioness in Ezek 19,5 at the deportation of her son. Job 14,19 gives the lament "you destroy the hope of a man". Ps 9,19 expresses trust in Yahweh, reflecting that the hope of the poor will not fail, while Prov 10,28; 11,7 and Job 8,13 announce that the hope of the wicked will perish. All these instances use both ʾBD and tiqwâ.

The parallels to the final phrase of the lament with the verb GZR are the most striking and illustrative. In Isa 53,8 the servant is said to be "cut off from the land of the living". The following verse mentions his tomb with the wicked. In Ps 88,6 the psalmist looks on himself as one lying in the tomb and thus as "cut off" from the hand of Yahweh. Lam 3,54-55 uses the expression "I am cut off", and cries to Yahweh from the deep pit. Thus the final expression of the lament in v.11b announces the idea of being condemned to the tomb and the pit, making the explicit talk of tombs in v.12 far from surprising.

Refutation

12   And so prophesy and say to them:
         thus says the Lord Yahweh:
         Look! I will open your tombs,
         and raise you from your tombs, my people,
         and bring you to the land of Israel.
13   And you will know that I am Yahweh,
         when I open your tombs
         and raise you from your tombs, my people.

In the face of dark despair Yahweh announces that he will open the tombs and raise his people from them. The refutation matches the hopelessness of the quotation with the stark image of the tomb. Even in such dire circumstances Yahweh will rescue them to return them to the land. The phrase "I will raise you from your tombs" echoes expressions of thanksgiving for rescue from the pit or Sheol in Ps 30,4 (ʿLH hiphil parallel to ḤYH piel); 40,3 (ʿLH hiphil parallel to QWM hiphil) and Jonah 2,7. Ps 71,20 more closely expresses confidence at expected deliverance from the depths of the earth (ḤYH piel parallel to ʿLH hiphil). The promised raising up of God's people from their tombs prepares for the promise of bringing them to their land, reminiscent of Ezek 20,42; 34,13; 36,24 and 37,21. The formula of recognition of Yahweh is extended in v.13b to restate the first two of Yahweh's promised actions, the opening of the tombs and the raising up of the people. The lack of repetition of the third action, the bringing back to the land, should not be considered surprising, since the refutation of the quotation necessarily concentrates on the opening of tombs and the raising up of the people in order to refute the words of the quotation. The people consider themselves condemned to the tomb. It is the first two acts of Yahweh which are important in the refutation of the quotation[138]. The people's lament of being condemned to the grave is thus countered by Yahweh's promise of liberation.

Conclusion

Form-critical considerations show clearly here that, although the vision and disputation speech have similar points to make, they are separate units and use different imagery. The disputation speech here is thus quite independent and only attached to the vision due to the similar message. The situation here is quite different from that in Ezek 11,1-13, where the disputation speech is an integral part of the vision and actually provokes the climax of the vision, the sudden death of Pelatiah[139].

Isaiah 40,27-31

Context, Structure and Unity

The question of the relationship of Isa 40,27-31 to the preceding verses, vv.12-26, is much debated. V.12-31 have often been divided into several small units[140]. A contrasting tendency is to regard vv.12-31 as a long poem, following what is thought to be a preference of Deutero-Isaiah for longer compositions and a free adaptation of genres[141]. At the same time doubts and hesitations have

---

[138] HOSSFELD, *Untersuchungen*, 367, by contrast, considers v.13b to be an addition since this extension to the formula of the recognition of God repeats only the first two actions of the three promised in v.12.

[139] HOEFFKEN, "Beobachtungen", 310-312, considers that the vision, 37,1-10, was expanded by an explanation from Yahweh (v.11a) and a disputation speech (vv.11b-12) to produce a text similar to Ezek 11, where visionary element (v.1), explanation by Yahweh (v.2), quotation (v.3) and related preaching (vv.4ff.) are again seen together. In fact, the nature of the relationship of disputation speech to vision in the two cases is quite different. In Ezek 37, an independent though thematically related disputation speech is tacked on to the vision in vv.1-11a. In Ezek 11,1-13, by contrast, the disputation speech (vv.2-12) is essential to the vision, for the death of Pelatiah in v.13 would be inexplicable without the prophet's speech. Furthermore, the "explanation" which Hoeffken finds in 11,2 is not an explanation of the whole vision, as it is in 37,11a.

[140] Thus BEGRICH, *Studien*; VON WALDOW, *Anlass und Hintergrund*; MELUGIN, *Isaiah 40-55*; ELLIGER, *Deuterojesaja*; MERENDINO, *Der Erste*. An account of their positions was given in the first part of this work and is summarised in the table on pp. 14-15.

frequently been apparent as to whether vv.12-31 are really a literary unit[142].

Isa 40,12-31 does in fact contain one disputation speech, with the basic elements of the genre, in vv.27-31. V.27 provides the introduction and quotation and vv.28-31 the refutation. The speech is complete in these verses. The structure found elsewhere reappears here. On form-critical grounds vv.27-31 appear to be a unit. It has been proposed, however, that vv.12-26 are a prelude to the disputation speech, and that vv.27-31 are the climax of vv.12-31. Three preliminary sections, vv.12-17; 18.21-24; 25-26, illustrate Yahweh's ability to help Israel, so that vv.27-31 can affirm his will to do so[143]. But these descriptions of the content of vv.12-26 and vv.27-31 are rather generic, and it must be considered whether such an understanding of these verses has not been imposed on the text in an attempt to demonstrate a dubious unity. The relationship of vv.12-26 to vv.27-31 needs closer examination.

The formal structure of the disputation speech begins in v.27, but this verse also shows a change of addressee. It is addressed to Jacob and Israel in the second person singular, whereas the second person plural was used in the preceding verses (vv.18.21.25.26). This might not necessarily be seen as the sign of a new unit, since it can be argued that in fact the addressees remain the same individuals[144]. However, there are several instances in Isa 40-48 where a unit begins with a second person singular address to Jacob and Israel, 41,8.14; 43,1.22; 44,1.21; 48,12. This suggests strongly that in 40,27 too a new unit is beginning.

---

[141] Thus, the unity of 40,12-31 is proposed by WESTERMANN, "Sprache und Struktur", 127-132, and *Jesaja*, 42. BONNARD, *Le Second Isaïe*, 96, considers the text a carefully constructed unit. MUILENBURG, *Isaiah 40-66*, 434, calls the verses a "hymnic monologue in the manner of a self-predication". McKENZIE, *Second Isaiah*, xxxiii, calls the text a "poem of creation". GITAY, *Prophecy and Persuasion*, 81-83, considers the verses a rhetorical unit, and states rather inaccurately that "vv.12-26 introduce the matter which is summarized in vv.27-31" (p. 82).

[142] WESTERMANN, *Jesaja*, 53, betrays some uncertainty in his conclusion on 40,12-31, affirming that the passage contains four disputations, but that only the last is the real disputation. SCHOORS, *God your Saviour*, 259, sees a perfect chiastic structure in vv.12-26, to which he adds 41,6-7 after v.20. He is not sure whether vv.12-26 were intended as a substructure for vv.27-31. WHYBRAY, *Isaiah 40-66*, 53, does not contest Westermann's view that vv.12-31 are a single composition, but at the same time affirms that each of its parts is complete and intelligible by itself. NAIDOFF, "Isaiah 40,12-31", 72-76, considers the text to be composed of four independent disputations, though he finds it impossible to say whether these ever existed independently. He lays great stress on how the four parts, seen together as a rhetorical whole, have the aim of encouraging the exiles.

[143] Thus WESTERMANN, "Sprache und Struktur", 127-132, and *Jesaja*, 42-43. Vv.19-20 are omitted as an addition by WESTERMANN, *Jesaja*, 47; McKENZIE, *Second Isaiah*, 24; ELLIGER, *Deuterojesaja*, 65-66, and others. SPYKERBOER, *The Structure and Composition*, 38-45, and CLIFFORD, "Idol Passages", 459-460, have defended vv.19-20 as an integral part of vv.12-31, but they do not face satisfactorily the question of the excessively technical nature of the verses and the resulting clash with the context. This makes it preferable to regard vv.19-20 as a gloss, perhaps due, as Elliger maintains, to a misunderstanding of *dᵉmût* in v.18 as a reference to concrete images. Clifford's division of the text into vv.12-17.18-24.25-31 completely disregards the fundamental importance of the quotation in v.27.

[144] MELUGIN, "Deutero-Isaiah and Form Criticism", 336, regards the change to the second person singular as the sign of a separate unit. SCHOORS, *God your Saviour*, 259, considers that the change from plural to singular "points to a separate unit". On the other hand, GITAY, *Prophecy and Persuasion*, 83, 85-86, suggests that the prophet is adopting a more intimate tone by speaking in the singular.

The difference in content also counsels a separation of vv.12-26 from vv.27-31. The three sections in vv.12-26 (vv.12-17; 18.21-24; 25-26) speak of Yahweh's incomparability: he is infinitely superior to the nations; the rulers of the earth are as nothing before him; he puts the stars through their paces. Vv.27-31 by contrast begin with words of the people and consider the practical issue of the readiness of Yahweh to help them[145].

Vocabulary links between vv.12-26 and vv.27-31 are not insignificant. The most important due to their central role in the refutation are two words denoting strength: *kōh* is found in v.26 and again in the refutation in vv.29.31; *'ônîm* similarly is found in v.26 and v.29[146]. On the other hand, whereas the three sections of vv.12-26 begin in vv.12.18.25 with rhetorical questions introduced by *mî* and *'el-mî*, v.27 introduces a genuine question with *lāmmâ*. The sequence in v.28 of *YD^c* and *ŠM^c*, echoed in v.21, is again found in 48,8. Similarity of vocabulary and expressions used can be explained generally by reference to Deutero-Isaiah's overall usage, and is not therefore a strong enough argument to challenge the separation of vv.27-31 from the preceding verses.

Vv.27-31 are an independent unit, principally because they display the complete disputation speech structure, and a change of addressee. The prophet uses here the regular structure of the disputation speech, as found in Jeremiah and Ezekiel.

Introduction and Quotation

27   Why do you say, Jacob,
        why do you repeat, Israel:
        My fate is hidden from Yahweh,
        by my God my just rights pass unnoticed?

The introduction takes the form of a direct question to those to whom the quotation is attributed. It is thus similar to Jer 8,8 "How can you say?" The addressing of the question to "Jacob" and "Israel" is the first time in Deutero-Isaiah that the exiles are addressed by the names of their ancestor.

Both clauses in the quotation, which displays a chiastic arrangement as in

---

[145] VOLZ, *Jesaia II*, 13, regarded vv.12-26 as theocentric and not designed to lead into the practical conclusion of vv.27-31. NORTH, *Second Isaiah*, 89, considers vv.12-26 present something similar to a cosmological argument and speak of the existence and creative power of Yahweh, which Israel never doubted. Vv.27-31, a quite separate unit, face the crucial question of God's concern for Israel's destiny.

[146] Less significant links of vocabulary between vv.12-26 and vv.27-31 concern for the most part words which are common in Deutero-Isaiah as a whole: *'ereṣ* (vv.12.21.22.24.28), *yhwh* (vv.13.27.28.31), *YD^c* (vv.13.14.21.28), *mišpaṭ* (vv.14.27), *derek* (vv.14.27), *t^ebûnâ* (vv.14.28), *ŠM^c* (vv.21.28), *NTN* (vv.23.29), *'MR* (vv.25.27), *BR'* (vv.26.28).

the quotation in Isa 49,14, are original expressions. The psalms often lament that Yahweh has hidden his face (as in Ps 10,11; 13,2; 30,8; 44,25; 88,15; 104,29), but here the expression is nearer to Job 3,23 "a man whose fate *(darkô)* is hidden *(nistārâ)*, whom God fences in". *derek* in the sense of "fate" is found of entrusting one's fate to God in Ps 37,5; the following v.6 then affirms that the same man's *mišpāṭ* will be brought out by Yahweh like the noon.

The second phrase expresses opposite sentiments to the trusting words of the servant in Isa 49,4, "my cause is with Yahweh". The "just rights" or "cause" of Israel, her *mišpāṭ*, is what God has promised her and is to be seen in relation to the "way of justice" which Yahweh lays down for all nations (40,14). Yahweh seems now to have no regard for Israel's position in his ordering of history[147]. Israel's just expectations have been passed over, just as Job's hope for salvation passes by like a cloud in Job 30,15. The originality of both expressions in this quotation, whether they arose from the people themselves or were simply attributed to them by the prophet, would seem to put in doubt any close relation to liturgical laments[148].

Refutation

28	Do you not know?
	Have you not heard?
	Yahweh is God of all time,
	the creator of the ends of the earth.
	He neither tires nor wearies,
	there is no penetrating his mind.
29	He gives the tired strength,
	and for him who has no force
	he redoubles his vigour.
30	Youths grow tired and weary,
	young men stumble and fall.
31	But those who hope in Yahweh renew their strength,
	they rise up on wings like eagles,
	they run and do not tire,
	they walk and do not weary.

The refutation begins with two rhetorical questions introduced by *hălô'*, reminiscent of the fourfold *hălô'* in 40,21. Yahweh is proclaimed as lord of all

---

[147] Thus ELLIGER, *Deuterojesaja*, 97, who sees *mišpāṭ* in 40,14 as referring to history in general, and in 40,27 as considering Israel's chosen position in that history.

[148] WESTERMANN, *Jesaja*, 51-52, suggests that the quotation here originated in liturgies of lament, and speaks of similarities with laments in Psalms and Lamentations. Contrast ELLIGER, *Deuterojesaja*, 97, who prefers to regard the words as originating among the people the prophet served.

time and creator of all[149]. The reference to Yahweh's impenetrable understanding is reminiscent of Ps 145,3; Job 5,9 and 9,10, which speak in similar terms of the great deeds of Yahweh.

The refutation approaches its principal point with the statement that Yahweh never tires nor wearies. From this point on the refutation is dominated by the two roots Y^cP (four times) and YG^c (three times), flanked by words from the semantic field of "strength". The description of Yahweh as one who does not tire is absolutely original here[150]. V.29 is the heart of the refutation. Yahweh who does not tire can thus give strength to the weary. The verse is dominated by the vocabulary of strength, $kōḥ$, $'ônîm$, $^coṣmâ$, as well as RBH. V.30, which describes how those who rely on human strength, even the young and vigorous, weary and fall, provides a powerful contrast to v.31, which affirms the constant reinvigoration of "those who hope in Yahweh"[151]. In the other disputation speech in Deutero-Isaiah, Isa 49,23 will affirm that "those who hope in Yahweh" will not be ashamed.

The statement "they rise up on wings like eagles" is again unparalleled. The nearest expression to it is perhaps in Ps 103,5, "your youth is renewed like the eagle's". $'ēber$ is to be taken as an accusative of instrument[152]. Those endowed with strength from Yahweh soar above difficulties, they run and walk without tiring. What was said of Yahweh in v.28, "he neither tires nor wearies", is said in conclusion of those who hope in Yahweh[153].

Conclusion

Isa 40,27-31 is a disputation speech similar to those in Jeremiah and Ezekiel. The introduction formulated as a question leads in a quotation expressing the people's despair, not unlike the despondent words uttered among the exiles and reported in Ezek 33,10 and 37,11b. The prophet sets against their dejec-

---

[149] The phrase "God of all time" is an effort to render the full sense of '*ôlām* as time both past, present and future, controlled by God. Thus also ELLIGER, *Deuterojesaja*, 98; JENNI, "*ôlām*," 239.

[150] V.28 uses novel expressions to describe Yahweh. It is difficult to justify WESTERMANN, *Jesaja*, 52, in his contention that the language of this verse is clearly that of the psalms of praise. He draws a parallel between vv.30-31a and Ps 33,16.18, but, while vaguely similar sentiments are expressed in the two texts, there is but one common word, *kōḥ*.

[151] V.30 concludes with a niphal verb strengthened by a qal infinitive absolute. JOÜON, *Grammaire*, 123 p.

[152] Thus NORTH, *Second Isaiah*, 34, renders: "they soar on eagle pinions". Contrast KNIGHT, *Deutero-Isaiah*, 43: "they shall put forth new pinions like eagles", or, more strangely, McKENZIE, *Second Isaiah*, 22: "they will sprout wings like eagles". These translations interpret as the LXX and Vg. However, in spite of the controversiality of the accusative of instrument (JOÜON, *Grammaire*, 126 1), and the misgivings of ELLIGER, *Deuterojesaja*, 101, the image of soaring on wings is to be preferred in the context to the idea of sprouting wings. The verb is thus qal.

[153] As ELLIGER, *Deuterojesaja*, 102, complains, WESTERMANN, *Jesaja*, 53, reads too much into the text when he maintains that v.31b introduces a new idea and alludes to the way back to Israel.

tion Yahweh's message of consolation. Deutero-Isaiah, like Ezekiel, uses the disputation speech structure to raise the exiles' spirits.

Isaiah 49,14-25

Context, Structure and Unity

That a new unit begins at Isa 49,14 is suggested by the quotation introduced there to be refuted in the succeeding verses. The refutation is dominated by words to Sion in the second person singular, in every verse except v.24. This clearly distinguishes the quotation and words of refutation both from what precedes and from what follows[154].

The internal structure of the passage reveals its exact extent. After the customary introduction and quotation in v.14 the refutation begins in v.15. This verse is a programmatic refutation, like those in Ezek 18,3-4; 20,33 and 33,11. While these verses are given weight by the oaths they contain, the programmatic refutation here gains in effect by being phrased as a rhetorical question and its solemn reply. But v.15 does not only serve to reject the quotation briefly while providing an anticipation of what is to come in the refutation. It also provides the framework to the refutation, corresponding closely in structure to vv.24-25. Just as v.15 provides a rhetorical question and reply, so too do vv.24-25, and both replies display the same grammatical structure of *gam... w^e...* While v.15 is a programmatic refutation, vv.24-25 can be described as a concluding refutation. The inclusion thus formed suggests that v.26 does not belong to the original unit, a suspicion which is confirmed by the harsh tone of the verse.

It is thus evident that after the quotation in v.14, v.15 and vv.24-25 form the framework for the refutation. The intermediate verses, vv.16-23, however, are also to be divided. The whole pericope is commonly divided into three sections, vv.14-20.21-23.24-26. Each section is considered as beginning with words of Sion[155]. But closer inspection reveals that the words in vv.14.21.24 are of differ-

---

[154] Volz, *Jesaia II*, 100, sees vv.7-26 as the unit. Muilenburg, *Isaiah 40-66*, 564, considers the introductory waw to be sufficient evidence to attach v.14 to what precedes. But in Ezek 20,32 another disputation speech begins with waw. McKenzie, *Second Isaiah*, 110-114, adds 50,1-3 to the unit. Bonnard, *Le Second Isaïe*, 217-218, considers Isa 49 to be a unit with three main parts, vv.1-6.7-13.14-26. By contrast, Merendino, "Jes 49,14-26", 323-324, sees four units in vv.14-26. He considers two of these units, vv.14-17.19b and vv.24-25, as the basic text, two units linked at an early stage in the complex history of composition of 49,14-26 (pp. 344-345). Merendino proposes the genre of his basic text to be "a kind of report of a court session" (p. 348).

[155] Westermann, "Sprache und Struktur", 120-121, 132-133, considers the three sections vv.14-20.21-23.24-26 to correspond to three parts of the liturgical lament: a lament against God, a lament in the first person, a lament concerning enemies. Yahweh answers each lament with words of salvation. Thus also Westermann, *Jesaja*, 177. Schoors, *God your Saviour*, 120-121, agrees with this analysis. Melugin, *Isaiah 40-55*, 149-151, criticises Westermann's analysis based on the lament psalm, and proposes to divide vv.14-21.22-23.24-26 as three salvation speeches, which belong closely together.

ing nature. V.14 of course is the opening quotation of Sion's words which trig-
gers off the disputation speech. V.21 quite clearly gives words of Sion, but these
words are not the beginning of a section, rather they are a reaction of Sion to
what precedes and in particular to what is announced as about to happen in
vv.17-20. The words Sion utters in v.21 are expressions of surprised delight at
her change in fortune. The time of lament is now past[156]. V.24 lastly, which
forms the first half of the concluding refutation and corresponds to v.15a, contains words which should be attributed not to Sion, but like v.15 to Yahweh[157].

Vv.16-23 are in fact to be divided after v.21. V.22 provides a messenger formula to introduce what is in fact the second refutation. It is followed by
hinnēh, which corresponds to *hēn* in v.16 at the beginning of the first refutation. The two refutations are thus vv.16-21 and vv.22-23. This division is confirmed by the content: while the first refutation announces the return of Sion's
sons, the departure of her oppressors and her consequent surprise and delight,
the second deals with the positive role played by the nations in bringing back
Sion's children and paying her homage.

Thus the developed structure of this disputation speech is as follows:

v.14 Introduction and Quotation

v.15 Programmatic Refutation
        rhetorical question with *hă*...
        reply with *gam*... *wᵉ*...

vv.16-21 First Refutation
        hēn...
vv.22-23 Second Refutation
        messenger formula
        hinnēh...

vv.24-25 Concluding Refutation
        rhetorical question with *hă*...
        reply with *gam*... *wᵉ*...

---

[156] SCHOORS, *God your Saviour*, 106-107, considers the two possibilities, that v.21 might look
backward or forward. V.22 with its messenger formula suggests v.21 goes with what precedes, but
v.21 contains a motif of lament. Schoors thus describes v.21 as a link between two proclamations of
salvation. His complete analysis (pp. 120-121), however, shows that he takes it principally as the opening lament of his second section (vv.21-23). V.21 does contain a lament, but a lament that is past, and
remembered by contrast with the present. It is the climax to vv.16-21, not the beginning of a new section.

[157] SCHOORS, *God your Saviour*, 114-116, considers the two possibilities, that v.24 is spoken by
Yahweh or is a lament of the people. He concludes that v.24 is a lament chiefly because he sees it as

Introduction and Quotation
14   But Sion said:
          Yahweh has abandoned me,
          my Lord has forgotten me.

The introduction beginning with consecutive waw seems to indicate a close relationship with what precedes. The words of Sion in fact mark a sharp contrast to the invitation to rejoicing in v.13.

The actual words of Sion's lament find their nearest parallel in Lam 5,20, which again uses ŠKḤ and ʿZB as parallel verbs. Ps 9,11-13 uses the same verbs in an expression of confidence in Yahweh, who neither abandons those who seek him, nor forgets the cry of the poor. As in Isa 40,27, the prophet gives expression here to the people's sense of having been abandoned by Yahweh.

Programmatic Refutation

15   Can a woman forget her suckling,
          and fail to cherish the child of her womb?
          Even if they were to forget,
          still I would not forget you.

The programmatic refutation is formulated as a rhetorical question followed by a reply. The reply is expressed as a conditional sentence with *gam... wᵉ...*, a construction which will return in vv.24-25. In the programmatic refutation the care of Yahweh for his people is compared to that of a mother for her baby; indeed, his care is greater[158]. The refutations will explain the programmatic refutation, showing the depths of Yahweh's love for his people.

First Refutation

16   Look! I have engraved you on my palms,
          your walls are always before me.
17   Your sons hasten to you,
          out from you will go those who overthrew you
          and laid you waste.

---

parallel to v.21, both verses beginning sections of the speech (vv.24-26.21-23) with laments. Once, however, it is seen that the lament in v.21 is not a starting-point but the climax of vv.16-21, the parallel with v.24 falls, and v.24 can be regarded, like v.15a on which it is modelled, as words of Yahweh.

    [158] *mᵉraḥēm* displays, as GKC 119 y indicates, a pregnant use of *min*, as seen again with the infinitive construct in Isa 5,6; 54,9; Lev 26,13. It is therefore unnecessary to correct to *mᵉraḥēm*, as suggested, among others, by Schoors, *God your Saviour*, 106, n. 2.

18   Raise your eyes around you and see,
          all of them have been gathered and have come to you.
          As I live, says Yahweh,
          you will be clothed with them all
          as with ornaments,
          like a bride you will bind them on.
19   For your ruins, your desolate places,
          your land with all its destruction,
          — now you will be too cramped for your inhabitants,
          and those who swallowed you up have gone far off.
20   They will yet say in your hearing,
          the children of your bereavement:
          The place is cramped for me,
          make room for me that I may dwell here.
21   You will say to yourself:
          Who bore me these?
          I was childless and barren,
          exiled and rejected,
          so who raised these?
          I was left quite alone,
          so where were these?

     The first refutation begins the illustration of how the great love of Yahweh
will transform Sion's condition. V.16 expresses with new images Yahweh's constant preoccupation for Sion. His care has two major effects. Those who op-
pressed Sion will depart (vv.17b.19b). The bulk of the refutation however
presents Sion herself as a bride and mother decking herself out with her
returning children as with ornaments[159]. Sion is told to raise her eyes and look
around her in v.18. Trito-Isaiah will use the same expression in 60,4, in the
same context of the return of Sion's children. The announcement of the return
is underlined by the oath formula "as I live" in v.18b. A frequent feature in
refutations in Ezekiel (18,3; 20,33; 33,11.27), it only appears here in Deutero-
Isaiah, in the refutation of a disputation speech[160]. V.19 describes how the land,
once desolate, now overflows with inhabitants. A similar description of the
numerous inhabitants of Sion is given in Isa 54,1-3.
     V.20 gives the words of the children who are so numerous as not to find

---

[159] In v.17 *bānāyik* is to be maintained. The alternative *bōnayik* is often preferred due to the contrast of "builders" and "destroyers" within v.17. But the contrast of the refutation as a whole is between the arrival of Sion's children and the departure of the enemy, as again in v.19b. The children are
repeatedly alluded to in vv.20-21, but there is no further word of building. This rejection of *bōnayik*
implies that another suggested alternative *mehōrᵉsāyik* is also to be rejected. *RSV* however adopts
both changes of vocalisation and renders: "your builders outstrip your destroyers".
[160] Isa 45,23 and 54,9 contain oaths of Yahweh with the verb *ŠBᶜ*.

sufficient space for their dwellings. The climax of the refutation, however, is reached in v.21, which admits the listener into Sion's private thoughts as she marvels at her change of fortune. Three questions, each with the astonished *'elleh*, two of them preceded by words describing Sion's previous state, bring the first refutation to a fine conclusion[161].

Second Refutation

22   Thus says the Lord Yahweh:
       Look! I raise my hand to the nations,
       and hoist my signal to the peoples,
       and they will bring your sons at their bosom,
       on their shoulders your daughters will be carried.
23   And kings will be your foster-fathers,
       and their princesses your nurses.
       Face to the ground they will pay you homage,
       they will lick the dust at your feet,
       and you will know that I am Yahweh,
       and that those who hope in me will not be ashamed.

The second refutation continues to describe how constant is Yahweh's care and compassion. This refutation, introduced formally with the messenger formula, has as its subject the positive role of the nations in assisting the return of Sion's children, and in coming themselves to pay her homage. It thus adds an even more amazing promise to what was announced in the first refutation.

Yahweh raises a signal to the nations to permit those who are scattered to return, as promised also in Isa 11,12. Vv.22-23 describe the assistance rendered by the nations. The nobles of the nations will finally prostrate themselves at Sion's feet, an event similar to those announced in Isa 45,14; 49,7 and 60,14, but more fully expressed here and with an atmosphere of reconciliation and peace between the nations.

The refutation ends with a variation on the formula of recognition of Yahweh, so often found in Ezekiel to conclude refutations or sections of them[162]. As in the other disputation speech in Deutero-Isaiah (40,31), the subject of the final verb is "those who hope in Yahweh". The message of the two speeches is similar. Even though Yahweh may seem to have abandoned and forgotten Israel, those who wait on him will be strengthened and saved.

---

[161] V.21 *gōlā w^esûrâ* is sometimes regarded as a gloss. Thus WESTERMANN, *Jesaja*, 176, n. 2; SCHOORS, *God your Saviour*, 108.

[162] Ezek 11,10.12; 20,38.42.44; 33,29; 37,13.

Concluding Refutation

24   Can booty be seized from a hero,
          or can captives escape from one who inspires awe?
25   For thus says Yahweh:
          Even if captives were to be seized from a hero,
          or booty escape from one who inspires awe,
          I would still oppose your adversary,
          and I would still save your children.

          In v.24 read ʿārîṣ for ṣaddîq due to v.25.

     The structure of vv.24-25 is identical to that of v.15, the programmatic
refutation. A rhetorical question introduced by hă is followed by a reply which
takes the form of a concessive conditional sentence where gam introduces the
protasis and wᵉ the apodosis. The only difference lies in the doubling of the
question to two clauses in v.24, introduced by hă... wᵉ'im...[163]. This leads to the
doubling of the protasis in the reply and a doubling of the apodosis follows; the
whole conditional structure is introduced by the messenger formula to give added emphasis to the conclusion of the unit[164]. The detailed structure of the programmatic and concluding refutations is thus as follows:

                    Programmatic Refutation

              v.15a hă + rhetorical question
              v.15b gam + protasis
                     wᵉ + apodosis including 'ānōkî

                    Concluding Refutation

              v.24 hă + rhetorical question
                    wᵉ'im + rhetorical question
              v.25 messenger formula
                    gam + protasis
                    wᵉ (û) + protasis
                    wᵉ + apodosis including 'ānōkî
                    wᵉ + apodosis including 'ānōkî

_____

[163] JOÜON, Grammaire, 161 e.

[164] There is no corresponding formula in v.15 to the messenger formula in v.25. This formula gives
added stress to Yahweh's final assurance that he will indeed come to his people's aid. It should not be
seen as a sign that v.24 which precedes should be attributed to the people rather than to Yahweh. Both
v.24 and v.25 are to be attributed to Yahweh. Contrast MERENDINO, "Jes 49,14-26", 341-342, who sees
v.24 as a genuine question, asked by Sion, to which v.25 is Yahweh's answer, introduced by the
messenger formula. Merendino attributes v.24 to Sion in spite of noting the similarity of v.24 to v.15a,
where Yahweh asks the question.

This similarity in structure suggests that vv.24-25 should also be translated in a similar manner to v.15[165]. In v.15a the rhetorical question in the first part of the verse invited a negative answer: no, mothers can never forget their children; v.15b then went on to say that even if this were to happen, which is quite inconceivable, Yahweh would still not forget Sion. Similarly in vv.24-25, the double rhetorical question in v.24 invited a negative reply: no, booty and captives cannot be taken from the hero or from the one who inspires awe; v.25 then goes on to say that even if these things were to happen, which is quite inconceivable, even in that abnormal turn of events, Yahweh would still oppose Sion's adversary and save her children[166]. Both in v.15 and v.25 Yahweh's intervention is stressed by *'ānōkî*.

This translation shows the full force of the inclusion with v.15 and brings the whole speech to a fine conclusion. But vv.24-25 have yet more to offer. In v.15 it was proposed that Yahweh was greater than a mother as regards his love for Israel. In vv.24-25, in parallel fashion, it is being suggested that Yahweh is greater than a hero or one who inspires awe in his defence of his people. Yahweh is in fact often referred to as *gibbôr*: Isa 42,13 sees him as going forth as a hero (*kaggibbôr*). Isa 9,5; 10,21; Jer 32,18; Ps 24,8; Deut 10,17 and Neh 9,32 use *gibbôr* with *'ēl* or *yhwh*. Jer 20,11 brings both attributes together when it says: "but Yahweh is with me as an awe-inspiring hero (*kᵉgibbôr ʿārîs*)". *ʿRS* also denotes Yahweh as awe-inspiring in Isa 8,12-13; 29,23 (hiphil) and Ps 89,8 (niphal). It could well be the relative strangeness of this description of Yahweh as *ʿārîs* which explains why in v.24 the text has been altered to *ṣaddîq*. A copyist who saw עריץ, especially if not clearly written, would be quite ready to read צדיק, a more "acceptable" designation for Yahweh (as in 45,21).

Thus while God is presented with qualities surpassing those of a mother in v.15, here he is greater than an awe-inspiring hero. It is both his tender love and his mighty strength which allow him to restore Israel to prosperity. V.15 and vv.24-25, which form an inclusion by structure for the two refutations, portray with two vivid images, that of mother and that of warrior, that Yahweh both wishes to and has the power to restore Sion and her children.

---

[165] V.25 is usually translated as four parallel affirmations, rather than as a conditional sentence. *RSV*: "Even the captives of the mighty shall be taken, and the prey of the tyrant be rescued, for I will contend with those who contend with you, and I will save your children." *TOB*: "Sûrement! la capture du héros sera reprise et la prise du tyran sera libérée! Ton querelleur, c'est moi qui vais le quereller; tes fils, c'est moi qui vais les sauver." WESTERMANN: "Wohl werden Gefangene dem Helden entrissen, und der Raub des Starken entkommt. Und mit deinen Streitern streite ich selber, und deinen Söhnen helfe ich selber." MUILENBURG, *Isaiah 40-66*, 577, surprisingly sees parallels between v.24 and v.14, and between vv.25-26 and vv.15-16. DUHM, *Jesaia*, 339, and McKENZIE, *Second Isaiah*, 111, render v.25 correctly as a conditional construction.

[166] "Awe-inspiring" is to be preferred to *RSV* "tyrant" for *ʿārîs*, since it conveys better the active sense of the word, based on the verb *ʿRS*.

Conclusion

The disputation speech in Isa 49,14-25 shows Deutero-Isaiah's skill in adapt-
ing the genre to his own purposes. Nevertheless, he maintains the structure in-
tact: the double refutation found in Ezekiel reappears here, and the formulae
common in Ezekiel, absent in Isa 40,27-31, return in v.18 (oath formula),
vv.22.25 (messenger formula) and v.23 (formula of recognition of Yahweh).
Deutero-Isaiah uses the structure of the genre for a poetic composition rich in
imagery, where the evocation of Yahweh as both mother and hero is matched in
the two refutations by the portrayal of the city Sion as both bride and mother.

Haggai 1,2.4-11

Unity and Structure

Hag 1,1 and 1,12-14 are generally considered the work of a redactor, v.1 giving the date and directing the first speech of the prophet to Zerubbabel the
governor and Joshua the high priest, and vv.12-14 narrating the reaction to the
prophet's words[167]. The actual speech, in vv.2-11, is a disputation speech,
though it has often been considered as composite and composed of a variety of
genres[168]. The structure of the passage is in fact similar to that of other
disputation speeches. V.2 gives the introduction and quotation[169]. A new and
cumbersome element is found in v.3, the formula of the coming of the word,
which would usually introduce a unit. This verse is not part of the original
speech, as further suggested by the phrase "by the prophet Haggai", and seems
to have been added by a redactor to ensure the speech was not seen as directed
to the leaders, as the redactional v.1 would suggest, but to the people, as a
direct reaction to their words in v.2[170]. V.4 is then the programmatic refutation,

---

[167] STECK, "Haggai 1,2-11", 356-357.
[168] ELLIGER, *Kleine Propheten*, II, 86, divides vv.4-11 into three sections, belonging to different
genres. HORST, *Kleine Propheten*, 205, finds three different speeches and one fragment in vv.2-11.
KOCH, "Haggais unreines Volk", 56-58, considers vv.2-8 to be the basic speech, a salvation speech, and
vv.9-11 a second saying on the same theme. The text is fragmented and assigned to different genres by
BEUKEN, *Haggai*. On p. 185 vv.4-6 and v.9 are described as disputation speeches, whereas on p. 186 and
p. 189 vv.4-6 are further divided into v.4 (an accusation) and vv.5-6 (a warning). While on pp. 187-188
vv.4-8 are a composite unit and v.9 and vv.10-11 two further units, on pp. 203-204 the original extent of
the prophetic speech is considered to be vv.4-10, which is described as an account of a prophetic intervention (*Auftrittsskizze*). WESTERMANN, Rezension BEUKEN, *Haggai*, 425-426, faced with the complex-
ity of Beuken's treatment, proposes a simple structure for the disputation speech. An account of this
is given in Part One, p. 20. STECK, "Haggai 1,2-11", 367-368, 371, finds a disputation speech (*Diskussionswort*) in vv.2.4-8, and a fragment of one in vv.9-11.
[169] The contention of ELLIGER, *Kleine Propheten*, II, 86, and BEUKEN, *Haggai*, 29-30, 204, n. 1, that
v.2 is a later addition, is quite unacceptable since the verse lays the foundation for the disputation
speech. AMSLER, *Aggée*, 23, similarly considers vv.1-2 to be the redactor's addition to explain the circumstances of the speech.
[170] Thus STECK, "Haggai 1,2-11", 360-361, n. 18.

which takes the form of a rhetorical question. The first refutation, vv.5-8, culminates in the command to gather wood and build the temple. Vv.9-11 are a second refutation in a more urgent tone.

Introduction and Quotation

2   Thus says Yahweh, the all-powerful:
         this people are saying:
         it is not the right time
         for the house of Yahweh to be built.
              ꜥet-bō' is to be omitted as dittography.

Haggai habitually refers to Yahweh with the title given here, as is shown in vv.5.7[171]. The designation of the speakers as "this people" is pejorative, as in Hag 2,14. The same title was given to the speakers in the disputation speech in Jer 33,24.

Various unsatisfactory attempts to preserve the MT of the quotation make it necessary to treat ꜥet-bō' as dittography[172]. The remaining quotation still has an unusual structure with ꜥet followed by the object built and a niphal infinitive. The regular mode of expression would be ꜥet followed by lᵉ and a qal infinitive (plus an object), as in 2 Kgs 5,26; Hos 10,12; Ps 119,126 and Qoh 3,2-8. Hag 1,4 also uses this more usual form.

Programmatic Refutation

4   Is it time for you yourselves to dwell
         in your panelled houses,
         while this house is in ruins?

The programmatic refutation is expressed as a rhetorical question, as in Isa 49,15. *lākem 'attem* stresses the contrast between the concern the people

---

[171] For the translation as an intensive abstract plural see EISSFELDT, "Jahwe Zebaoth", 110-113. VAN DER WOUDE, "ṣābā'", 503-507, gives a survey of three principal translations, and considers Eissfeldt's the most likely.

[172] ELLIGER, *Kleine Propheten*, II, 85, and HORST, *Kleine Propheten*, 204, correct to ꜥattā bā', but, as STECK, "Haggai 1,2-11", 361-362, n. 21, points out, Haggai usually uses ꜥattâ (1,5; 2,3.4.15) and the resulting syntax is doubtful. ACKROYD, *Exile*, 155, n. 8, suggests "time to cóme (in)" as a translation and sees the phrase as a possible reference to religious ceremonies. This interpretation, however, seems excluded by the reply which concerns only the building of the temple, and rather remote from the specific context of the speech.

show for themselves and that shown for Yahweh[173]. The rendering of *sāpûn* as "panelled" rather than "roofed" fits better with the intended sharp contrast between the excessive concern of the people for their own houses, and their lack of attention to the house of Yahweh. *SPN* is found in a similar critical tone in Jer 22,14, where the prophet attacks Jehoiakim's grandiose building plans, which include cedar panelling[174]. The rhetorical question in this programmatic refutation already implies that it is indeed time to build Yahweh's house. The refutation will offer proof of this.

First Refutation

5   And now thus says Yahweh, the all-powerful:
           Consider your situation.
6   You sowed in abundance, and brought in little,
           you eat and do not have your fill,
           you drink and remain unsatisfied,
           you clothe yourselves and do not feel warm.
           The wage-earner earns wages
           for a purse full of holes.
7   Thus says Yahweh, the all-powerful:
           Consider your situation.
8   Go up to the hill country and bring wood,
           and build the house,
           and I will take pleasure in it,
           and display my glory, says Yahweh.

A similar expression to the exhortation "consider your situation" in 1,5.7 is to be found in 2,15.18, where the people are told to look to the future. The prophet insists here that the people take stock of their plight and reflect on what has caused it. Only then will they have the will to obey the commands of v.8 and begin work on the house of Yahweh. The position of the second call to "consider your situation" in v.7b has been contested [175]. But the MT is best maintained as it stands. The insistence that the people consider seriously their present state prepares them to accept the command which follows directly in v.8,

---

[173] GKC 135 g and JOÜON, *Grammaire*, 146 d, explain the personal pronoun following the preposition with suffix as giving special emphasis.

[174] ELLIGER, *Kleine Propheten*, II, 85; HORST, *Kleine Propheten*, 204; RUDOLPH, *Haggai*, 29, render "panelled". As AMSLER, *Aggée*, 24, suggests, the tone of the verse allows for some exaggeration. It is not necessary to consider that, especially in the circumstances of need described later, all the people had luxuriously decorated houses. By contrast, STECK, "Haggai 1,2-11", 362, prefers to translate "roofed", which considerably weakens the force of the verse.

[175] ELLIGER, *Kleine Propheten*, II, 86, considers v. 7b a mistake. BEUKEN, *Haggai*, 186, n. 3, rejects v.7b as an interruption. AMSLER, *Aggée*, 21-22, suggests it should be placed after v.8.

and to acknowledge that the words of their quotation were wrong[176]. The refutation does not state explicitly that failure to build the temple has led to the disastrous conditions reported in v.6, but by insisting that the people consider their situation before giving the explicit call to rebuild the temple the prophet obviously wishes them to draw this conclusion[177].

V.6 contains a certain amount of material similar to that found in OT curses. The people are eating and not being satisfied. Lev 26,26 lays this down as part of the punishment for continued defiance of Yahweh. Hos 4,10 announces a similar fate for the priests, and Mic 6,14 gives the same threat against the wicked. Deut 28,38 lists poor returns for abundant sowing among the curses which will punish the people's infidelity. The people addressed in this disputation speech are suffering from such curses[178]. There are however no parallels regarding clothing and not feeling warm, and v.6b is an eloquent and original complaint against rising prices. Similarity with material found in OT curses is thus limited. Furthermore, such material is not used here in order to deliver a curse or threat. It is used rather to describe the actual situation in which the people seem to be suffering the effects of a curse[179]. The use of curse material to describe the situation and as a response to the quotation in v.2 implies that those words were wrong, and that consequently it is indeed time to rebuild the house of Yahweh.

The climax of the first refutation, prepared for by the messenger formula and renewed call to the people to consider their plight in v.7, comes in v.8 with the practical command to go to the hills, bring wood and begin to build. In no other disputation speech was there such a practical consequence to the refutation of the people's words, though the imperatives here might be compared to the imperatives calling for repentance in Ezek 33,11. However, the basic point of the speech is still to confront an erroneous opinion and refute it. Disregard for Yahweh's house has led to Yahweh's displeasure. It is therefore surely time for the people to admit they were wrong and begin building. As if to confirm that the remedy lies in rebuilding the temple Yahweh announces that he will take pleasure in it and display his glory. $RṢH$ b^e is used both of Yahweh's

---

[176] RUDOLPH, *Haggai*, 34, n. 21, defends the repetition, but is not justified in affirming that whereas v.5 is directed to the past and the present, v.7 looks to the future. V.7 in fact insists that the people consider their present state so that they will realise that by obeying the commands of v.8 they will be able to put the situation to rights.

[177] Similarly STECK, "Haggai 1,2-11", 363-364, n. 30.

[178] BEUKEN, *Haggai*, 192, n. 1, gives an exhaustive list of curses, mostly corresponding to those found in HILLERS, *Treaty-Curses*, 29.

[179] BEUKEN, *Haggai*, 196-197, is thus inaccurate in referring to the use of the genre of curse. As STECK, "Haggai 1,2-11", 364-365, explains, the material similar to that found in curses is used not to express a curse but to call attention to the present lack of blessing due to the fact that the temple has not been rebuilt. RUDOLPH, *Haggai*, 34, considers that the statements in v.6 simply mirror the harsh reality of life at the time.

pleasure in his people (Ps149,4) and in things (Mic 6,7;Ps 147,10)[180]. *KBD* in the niphal used of God has a reflexive rather than a passive sense: God himself shows his glory, as in Exod 14,4.17.18; Isa 26,15; 66,5 (corrected text); Ezek 28,22 and 39,13[181]. This could well be seen as announcing the return of God to dwell in his temple. The end of the refutation is marked by the brief formula, *'āmar yhwh*.

Second Refutation

9   You are occupied with many things
         but produce little,
         you bring it home and I blow on it.
         Why? says Yahweh, the all-powerful.
         Because of my house which is in ruins,
         while each of you runs off to his own house.
10   Therefore it is due to you
         that the heavens withheld the dew,
         and the land withheld its yield.
11   And I called down drought on the land,
         on the hills,
         on the corn, on the wine, on the oil,
         and on what the soil produces,
         on man and beast,
         and on all the produce of man's hands.

The second refutation is given in a more urgent tone. There is no introduction and only one formula to stress the rhetorical question asked by Yahweh in v.9b. V.11 excitedly accumulates a long list of victims of the judgement Yahweh himself had decreed, a judgement arising from the people's preoccupation with their own houses while they neglected the house of Yahweh. The second refutation stresses the disastrous effects of the people's neglect of Yahweh but does not spell out the practical remedy. This is already clear from v.8a.

V.9a tells again of the contrast between the people's efforts and the poor results realised. Furthermore, whatever is brought in from the harvest is quickly ruined by Yahweh. It has been proposed that the house to which the produce is brought is the temple: in spite of its ruined state the people still bring offerings to the site of the temple, but these are not accepted by Yahweh[182]. *bayit* in

---

[180] GERLEMAN, "*rṣh*", 811.
[181] WESTERMANN, "*kbd*", 801.
[182] Thus PETER, "Haggai 1,9", 150-151. Also ACKROYD, *Exile*, 158, and STECK, "Haggai 1,2-11", 370, n.46.

this disputation speech refers predominantly to the temple (vv.2.4.8.9), but it is also used for the houses of the people (vv.4.9), and this is the rendering that fits the context better. What is being said, in parallel to v.6, is not that offerings made on the site of the ruined temple are unacceptable, but that the little the people manage to produce and take home lies under the curse of Yahweh, precisely because they are not in the least concerned about sacrifices to Yahweh and the rebuilding of his house[183]. The expression "I blow on it" seems close in sense to the hiphil of *NPḤ* in Mal 1,13, which expresses the people's disdain for offering sacrifices[184]. In v.9b Yahweh questions the people rhetorically as to the reason for their plight and himself gives the answer: his own house is in ruins while each of them "runs off to his own house"[185]. "House" can be understood in the broader sense of each man's household and the affairs concerning it[186].

Vv.10-11 describe the punishment inflicted by Yahweh due to the people's neglect in stronger terms than those used in v.6. There is no room for doubt that the calamities are "due to you"[187]. The whole of creation, heaven and earth, does not function normally. And Yahweh has called down a drought on a long list of victims[188]. Such a long list might have been added to in the course of redaction. But such lists are not unknown and to be found particularly in Jeremiah's announcements of punishments. In Jer 7,20 Yahweh's wrath is kindled against man and beast, as here, but also against the trees of the plain and the fruit of the land. Jer 9,24-25 gives an even longer sequence of victims, nations circumcised only in the flesh, to be punished by Yahweh, again each one introduced by *ʿal*. Jer 25,9 provides a list of the victims of Nebuchadnezzar, while v.12 lists him among the victims. Jer 31,12 by contrast lists the corn, the wine, the oil and the offspring of sheep and cattle as reasons for rejoicing, but again with multiple *ʿal*. Exod 7,19 and 9,22 list the victims of the plagues

---

[183] BEUKEN, *Haggai*, 187-188, n. 1. For RUDOLPH, *Haggai*, 29-30, the content of the beginning of v.9 shows the context is not cultic.

[184] RUDOLPH, *Haggai*, 35, n. 22, sees any reference here to magic power to be quite improbable with Yahweh as subject.

[185] STECK, "Haggai 1,2-11", 370, interprets this verse as meaning that the people concerned in vv.9-11 do not yet have their own houses, and are therefore a different group from those addressed in vv.2-8. But the prophet would hardly be justified in attacking them so vehemently in vv.9-11 if they did not yet have shelter. The attack is vehement precisely because each one is concerned exclusively with his own affairs and has neglected the worship of Yahweh. RUDOLPH, *Haggai*, 36, points out the inadequacies of Steck's interpretation. There is no sign in v.9 that the people addressed are any different, and in vv.12-14 the people are seen as one group in their reaction to the prophet's speech.

[186] ACKROYD, *Exile*, 158, n. 22; RUDOLPH, *Haggai*, 35-36.

[187] STECK, "Haggai 1,2-11", 369, and AMSLER, *Aggée*, 22, render *ʿalêkem* "upon you". Amsler maintains that the rendering "due to you" would be pleonastic. In fact "due to you" makes *ʿal-kēn* "therefore" absolutely explicit to leave no doubt in the listeners' minds that they are responsible. RUDOLPH, *Haggai*, 30, renders "due to you", and considers that the expression introduces also v.10b and v.11, which makes the translation "upon you" unacceptable.

[188] RUDOLPH, *Haggai*, 36, n. 24, notes how the drought (*ḥōreb*) is fitting punishment for the fact that the temple is still in ruins (*ḥārēb*).

wrought by Yahweh against the Egyptians. Deut 7,13, on the other hand, announces a group of recipients of Yahweh's blessing without ʿal, but which includes the fruit of the soil, corn, wine and oil. Such lists of recipients of curse or blessing suggest that the whole of v.11 should be treated as part of the original text[189].

The second refutation thus lays even greater stress than the first on the consequences of the people's disregard for Yahweh. It does not reiterate the solution, already given in v.8a in the first refutation, but it spells out explicitly for the first time in v.9b the reason for the dire conditions. Yahweh asks what the reason is. The reason is the neglect of his house. In this way the two refutations leave nothing unsaid. They both stress the effects of not building the temple, and while the first gives the solution in v.8a, the second provides the reason already implied, stating it unequivocally in v.9b.

Conclusion

The developed structure of the disputation speech, with two refutations, as found in Ezekiel and Deutero-Isaiah, warns against dividing this disputation speech into separate units. The basic difference between the two refutations is one of tone: the calm tone of the first refutation gives way to a more urgent and excited manner of speech in the second, seen particularly in the impatient questioning in v.9 and the emphasis on the full toll of the disastrous effects of not building the temple in vv.10-11.

---

[189] BEUKEN, *Haggai*, 201-202, considers v.11 an addition to complete the speech.

PART THREE

Concluding Observations
and a Suggestion

The use of structure as the starting-point has led to a clarification of a literary genre (Section 1). An overall view can now be given of the various elements of the genre (Section 2), and its setting in the life of ancient Israel can be described (Section 3). Finally, it is proposed that Jesus too used the genre (Section 4).

1. Methodological Note

This study set out to investigate the prophetic device of quoting the people's words in order to refute them. A major result of the investigation is the provision of clear and acceptable criteria for assigning a prophetic speech to the literary genre "disputation speech". The first part of the study gave ample illustration of the variety of texts assigned to the genre and of the lack of established and accepted criteria. The basic criterion proposed is that of formal structure. The structure consists of two chief parts, the quotation of the people's opinion and the refutation which corrects this opinion. By no means all the texts proposed elsewhere as disputation speeches display this structure, but where the structure is found an explicit repudiation of a mistaken opinion is genuinely present. Only texts with this structure are to be called "disputation speeches". They are to be distinguished from "disputations" or "dialogue disputations", which report a dispute in direct speech, for in the disputation speech it is the prophet himself who conveys the opposing view (pp.9-10). The traditional name "disputation speech" is preserved, but refers to the genre in which the prophet sets out with the explicit intention of refuting an erroneous statement which he himself reports. The designation thus has a more restricted use, but becomes more precise and consequently more useful.

The syntactical form of the speeches consists of an introduction with the verb 'MR which leads in the quotation, which in turn is followed by the refutation. The consideration of the syntactical form permits an understanding of the inner dynamics of the text, the process of formally putting forward a view which is then refuted. The inner working of the text is revealed by judicious isolation of syntactical and stylistic elements with significant functions in the unit. In proposing a formal structure for the disputation speech the specific content of the individual texts was not considered. Indeed, the establishment of the formal structure of the text was a prerequisite for a correct approach to the content. A fine example of how a correct grasp of structure leads to a correct interpretation of a text was seen in Ezek 33,17.20. The rejoinder of the people given here is a development of the basic structure of the disputation speech, found also in Ezek 18,19. A grasp of the role of Ezek 33,17.20 within the structure of the disputation speech raised doubts about the suitability of the traditional translation as "the way of the Lord is not just". Investigation of the use of the verb *TKN* in the MT confirmed that a translation fitting better in the context was available (pp.76-77). Thus correct interpretation was seen to flow from a precise grasp of the structure.

Consideration of the structure of a unit leads to an understanding of the aim of the text and to the establishment of the genre. This principle allowed a clear separation of Jer 33,23-26 from two texts with similar content, Jer 31,35-37 and 33,19-22. The structure of quotation and refutation in Jer 33,23-26 showed that the aim of the text was to refute the people's opinion. It is thus of a different genre from the other texts, where no contrary opinion is apparent (p.39). Taking content as the criterion for genre would have led to an indiscriminate lumping together of all three texts.

By taking note of formal structure, and prescinding from content until the genre was established, it has been possible to provide a precise idea of the genre "disputation speech". This study may be seen as a vindication of the contention of W. Richter that the examination of structure is the necessary starting-point for the establishment of the genre of a particular unit. Richter suggests two stages of genre criticism, "comparison of structure" and "genre designation"[1]. Richter's position is not one of total disregard for the content of the text until the final stage of his method, but the mode of expression must be abstracted to facilitate a true understanding of the form and thus the aim of the unit. Content is considered at this stage not in its specificity, but in order to abstract elements of form significant in the functioning of the text, common elements which are found in several units which belong to the same genre.

In his study of the reproach (*Scheltwort*) in Amos, L. Markert accepts the general lines of Richter's method, but seeks to avoid seeing form and content in opposition to each other[2]. Markert thus proposes to distinguish between the mode of expression (*Ausdrucksseite*) and the meaning (*Bedeutungsseite*) in an at-

---

[1] RICHTER, *Exegese*, 131-141. A brief account of Richter's approach to genre criticism is given in GRAFFY, "Isaiah 5,1-7", 400-401.

[2] MARKERT, *Struktur und Bezeichnung*, 285, n. 15. RICHTER, *Exegese*, 33, n. 18, suggests seeing form and content in opposition to each other. Richter's statement here is misleading. One might contrast it with a later statement on p. 78, where form and content are seen as inter-dependent.

tempt to establish a middle way between Richter and his critics[3]. However, it is hard to see how this position differs from Richter's, who himself distinguished the mode of expression (*Ausdrucksseite*) from the content or message (*Inhaltsseite*)[4].

Richter's attempt to provide a methodology for OT exegesis has been criticised for its strictness. Knierim calls for more flexibility in defining what constitutes a genre, and advocates a multiplicity of methods[5]. Koch contests the strict order of separate stages in the method[6]. It would seem that it is precisely too much flexibility and a laxity of method which led to the prevailing lack of clarity in the treatment of the disputation speech. Kaiser prefers to reserve judgement concerning Richter's stress on formal analysis as a stage of his method since it is still in an experimental stage[7]. H. Barth and O. H. Steck strenuously oppose Richter's separation of form and content and stress his neglect of the historical dimension of the text by his initial disregard for content[8]. C. Hardmeier considers that Richter has provided no theory to justify the separate treatment of form and content[9].

The discussion regarding the theoretical justification for a separate treatment of content and form will surely continue. But a method is vindicated when it achieves satisfactory results. In this instance the examination of the structure of certain prophetic speeches has served to reveal their common aim, and thus led to a correct understanding of their specific content. The method starting from a comparison of structure has led to a clarification of what the texts have in common, and to a more precise understanding of a prophetic genre.

2. The Parts of the Disputation Speech

The individual disputation speeches have already been analysed in accordance with the structure of quotation and refutation, the proposed criterion for designation as a disputation speech. It is now possible to give a comprehensive account of the various elements of the genre.

The Introduction (see the table on p.116)

The genre consists of two principal parts, the quotation and the refutation.

---

[3] MARKERT, *Struktur und Bezeichnung*, 287-289.
[4] RICHTER, *Exegese*, 32, 78, 119.
[5] KNIERIM, "Form Criticism", 447, 468.
[6] KOCH, *Formgeschichte*, [3rd edition] 331-332.
[7] KAISER, *Einführung*, 26-27.
[8] BARTH, STECK, *Exegese*, 57-58, n. 84, 74-76.
[9] HARDMEIER, *Texttheorie*, 47-48, n. 76.

The quotation is preceded, however, by a formal introduction. All the speeches showing the quotation-refutation pattern are preceded by a formal introduction. In fact, common elements found either in all disputation speeches, or in significant groups of them, are more numerous here than in the quotations or refutations.

A dominant formal element in the introduction to the disputation speech is the formula of the coming of the word, "the word of Yahweh came to me saying". Besides Jer 33,23, it is found in five of the nine disputation speeches of Ezekiel. It is lacking in the other four due to the close relationship of these speeches to what precedes. In Ezek 11,2 the disputation speech begins simply with "And he said to me", for it is inserted in a vision (p.42). Ezek 20,32-44 serves to counterbalance vv.1-31, and the formula of the coming of the word in v.2 introduces both speeches (pp. 65-66). Similarly, the formula in Ezek 33,1 serves both vv.1-9 and the disputation speech in vv.10-20, two closely related units (p.72). Ezek 37,11b-13 is added to vv.1-11a due to the theme of dry bones. A simple introduction, "they are saying" in v.11b, suffices, but this is attached to Yahweh's words explaining the vision in v.11a, and thus becomes part of Yahweh's speech (pp.83-84). When present, the formula of the coming of the word makes quite clear that it is Yahweh who informs the prophet of the people's words. But this is the case in all Ezekiel's disputation speeches, even where the formula is absent. Yahweh takes the initiative and upbraids the prophet over the quotation. In Hag 1,2 too Yahweh informs the prophet of the quotation. Here it is the messenger formula which introduces the speech: "Thus says Yahweh, the all-powerful: this people are saying". On occasion Yahweh even displays indignation at the quotation of which he is informing the prophet. In Jer 33,24 he asks, "Have you not noticed what this people has said?" In Ezek 12,22 and 18,2 there are similar indignant questions. With Jer 8,8 and Isa 40,27, on the other hand, it is the prophet who challenges the people directly over their words. Jer 8,8 begins simply with "how can you say?" and Isa 40,27 with "why do you say, Jacob, why do you repeat, Israel?".

The principal verb used in almost all the introductions to the quotations in disputation speeches is *'MR*. Even on the few occasions where another verb is used, the form *lē'mōr* is added. Thus Ezek 12,22 and 18,2 use the root *MŠL* with *lē'mōr*, and Jer 33,24 uses *lē'mōr* with the verb *DBR*. Isa 40,27 has *'MR* and *DBR* in parallel hemistichs. Thus it is a characteristic of the disputation speech that the formal introduction always contains some form of *'MR*.

The main verb introducing the quotation is found in various forms. In Ezekiel it is the participle which predominates, though the qatal is found in 11,15 and 33,10. Outside Ezekiel the participle is not found. The yiqtol is used in Jer 8,8; 31,29 and Isa 40,27, while the qatal appears in Isa 28,15; Jer 33,24 and Hag 1,2. The use of the participle and yiqtol would seem to stress a repeated use of the quotation. Isa 49,14 has a unique *wattō'mer*, which emphasises the contrast of Sion's coming words with the jubilation which preceded in v.13 (p.93).

The immediate introduction to the quotation is usually in the form of a statement such as "this people says" or "you say". But it can be expressed as a question about the quotation, either to the prophet, as in Jer 33,24; Ezek 12,22 and 18,2, or to the people, as in Jer 8,8 and Isa 40,27. The formulation as a question attracts the verb to the second person, except in Jer 33,24, where the question with *DBR* is indirect. Formulation as a statement is usually in the third person, except in Isa 28,15; Ezek 20,32 and 33,10, where the statement is in the second person plural.

Another component of the introduction to the disputation speech is the subject of the principal verb, *'MR* or its substitutes. This subject can sometimes be contained in the verb, as in Isa 28,15; Jer 8,8; 31,29; Ezek 33,10; 37,11b and Isa 40,27, or signified by a pronoun, as in Ezek 18,2 and 20,32. But the speakers of the quotation may be described at greater length: the "inhabitants of Jerusalem" in Ezek 11,15; the "house of Israel" in Ezek 12,27; the "inhabitants of these ruins" in Ezek 33,24. The description of the speakers becomes pejorative in Jer 33,24 with "this people" (p.39), as also in Hag 1,2 (p.99). In Isa 28,14 and Ezek 11,2 a fuller and highly negative description of the speakers is given in the introduction. In Isa 28,14 they are "men of arrogance, who lay down the law for this people in Jerusalem". In Ezek 11,2 they are those "who contrive iniquity, who plan plans of evil in this city". In these latter cases the negative description of the speakers casts a shadow on their words even before they speak. Isa 49,14, by contrast, makes Sion, the personified city, the speaker of the quotation. Finally, Ezek 11,15 is exceptional in giving a lengthy description of the people about whom the quotation has been coined, "your brothers, your kinsmen and the whole house of Israel".

Special attention must be paid to two particular introductions, which do more than simply introduce the quotation. Ezek 20,32 stresses that the idea expressed by the quotation "shall certainly not come to pass". This original introduction rejects the validity of the quotation categorically even before the refutation begins. A similarly original text is Jer 31,29-30. The introduction announces that "in those days they will no longer say" the quotation. One might consider that what is announced here is primarily a promise for the future, introduced as it is by "in those days". However, several factors counsel seeing the unit as a disputation speech. The quotation is almost identical with that in Ezek 18,2, where a lengthier disputation speech begins. This suggests that a disputation speech may be present in Jeremiah too. A new quotation is substituted for the old in Jer 31,29-30. This technique is used also in the disputation speech, Ezek 12,21-25. This is a stronger indication that Jer 31,29-30 is a disputation speech. But the most important factor is that all the essentials of the structure of the disputation speech are present in Jer 31,29-30. The text sets out to correct a false opinion, which is the characteristic aim of the disputation speech (p.36). Nevertheless, it must be admitted that Jer 31,29-30 is a case in which it is the task of the investigator to make the final careful decision regarding genre.

The Quotation (see the table on p.117)

The introductions showed significant common elements, even if they were usually shared only by some of the disputation speeches. In the quotations, by contrast, the similarities are minimal, for there are fewer constraints on the content. Only in the refutations will a certain formal similarity again be apparent.

On the grammatical and syntactical level there is a wide variety of forms in the quotations. Verbs and pronouns, as might be expected, are predominantly in the first and third persons, the second person never being found.

The quotations usually consist of two principal clauses. Those in Ezek 20,32 and Hag 1,2 are exceptions in having only one clause, though in both the clause is extended by l^e with an infinitive construct. The relationship between the clauses can be one of synonymous parallelism, as is the case in Ezek 12,27; Isa 40,27 and 49,14. Alternatively, a logical link may exist between the two clauses. In Jer 8,8 it is due to their possession of the Law that the people consider themselves wise. The claim to the land in Ezek 11,15 gives the exiles' banishment as its reason. In Ezek 12,22 the passing days substantiate the view that there is nothing to fear from the prophecies of disaster. Three clauses are found in the lamenting quotations in Ezek 33,10 and 37,11b. The quotation in Ezek 33,24 is more extensive, consisting of two parallel statements, with two clauses each. The whole forms an "a minori ad maius" argument. Isa 28,15 has the longest quotation, consisting of six clauses: two reasons for confidence precede and two follow the central statement of confidence, itself comprising two clauses (p.26).

Chiastic links often bind the quotations together. Simple chiasms are found in Ezek 12,27; Isa 40,27 and 49,14. In Ezek 33,24 a double chiastic link binds the two clauses in the first statement to the corresponding clauses in the second, protasis to protasis, and apodosis to apodosis. In Isa 28,15 there is a chiastic layout in the reasons for confidence which both precede and follow the central statement of the quotation.

The Explanatory and Preparatory Remarks

Material additional to the basic structure is found after the quotation in Jer 33,24b and Ezek 11,4-6. These verses in no way place in jeopardy the basic structure of the disputation speeches. Jer 33,24b consists of a comment on the quotation by Yahweh himself and is thus designated an "explanatory remark" (p.40). The material in Ezek 11,4-6, on the other hand, looks forward to the refutations, the first of which begins with the messenger formula in v.7. Vv.4-6 contain a continuation of Yahweh's speech and a narrative parenthesis. The verses are designated "preparatory remarks" since they build up the expectation for the refutations to come (pp.44-45).

The Refutation (see the table on p.117)

The name "refutation" was chosen for the second principal element of the disputation speech in order to include the varied ways in which the quotation can be rejected. A refutation may explicitly take up a statement from the quotation and deny it. The words of the quotation in Isa 28,15, "the overflowing flood, when it passes, will not reach us", are explicitly rejected in v.18, "the overflowing flood will indeed pass, and you will be trampled by it". In Ezek 11,2-12 different parts of the quotation, "this is the pot, and we are the meat", are explicitly denied in the two refutations. In v.7 it is the victims murdered by the leaders of the people who are the meat, and in v.11 it is denied that the city will be a pot to protect the people. In Ezek 33,25-26 rhetorical questions take up the claim of the quotation explicitly.

But the refutation is more than a denial of the quotation. It gives reasons for rejecting the quotation, reasons which frequently include the announcement of a future intervention by Yahweh. Thus it is not surprising that the yiqtol and weqatalti forms of the verb are the most common, for in almost every disputation speech Yahweh's coming intervention is announced, and usually in the first person. There are a few refutations where the first person with Yahweh as subject does not appear, but even in these Yahweh is understood to be planning action. In Jer 8,8-9 a punishment is announced in the refutation; though an intervention of Yahweh is not explicitly mentioned, it can be presumed that it was Yahweh who decreed the punishment. In Isa 40,27-31 Yahweh's will to save is proclaimed. In Ezek 18,1-20 it is Yahweh's rule of conduct in judgement, "it is the person who sins that shall die" (v.4), which provides the basis of the refutation of the quotation. No act of Yahweh is announced in Jer 31,29-30, but the people's proper understanding of how he acts is promised (p.37). It can be said that the refutation either considers how Yahweh acts habitually, as in Jer 31,29-30; Ezek 18,1-20 (that he punishes individually) and Ezek 33,10-20 (that he wants the sinner to live), or announces what he plans in the future. In Hag 1,2.4-11, where attention is repeatedly concentrated in the refutations on the actual plight of the people due to Yahweh's displeasure, and where it is this which ought to convince them of the erroneousness of their quotation, the goal of rebuilding the temple is that "I will take pleasure in it (the house), and display my glory" (v.8). Fundamental to every refutation therefore is a consideration of Yahweh's action, habitual or expected, the announcement of which implies the falsity of the quotation.

The refutation by definition represents a challenge to the people's words. It is therefore understandable that this part of the disputation speech should begin with the messenger formula, announcing that Yahweh thinks differently from the people. This is in fact the case in the majority of disputation speeches. In Ezekiel the formula usually begins the refutations. In 18,3; 20,33 and 33,11 it is replaced by the oath formula *hay-'ānî* in programmatic refutations. Only in 11,11, which is the second rejection of the quotation in 11,3, does no formula whatsoever introduce the refutation. Outside Ezekiel, the messenger formula begins refutations in Isa 28,16; Jer 33,25; Isa 49,22 and Hag 1,5. But it can also be found within a refutation to give special stress. In Ezek 20,39 the messenger formula leads in the command to do away with idols (p.71). It stresses Yahweh's final words in Isa 49,25 (p.96). In Hag 1,7 it prepares for the command to rebuild the temple in v.8, the climax of the first refutation (p.101). The messenger formula generally emphasises that the denial of the quotation is from Yahweh; he will prove the quotation wrong by his own actions.

The oath formula *hay-'ānî*, reinforced usually by *ne'um 'ǎdōnāy yhwh*, is another device which stresses Yahweh's rejection of the quotation. It is found in programmatic refutations in Ezek 18,3; 20,33 and 33,11 and beginning the second refutation in Ezek 33,27. In Isa 49,18 it appears later in the refutation. The particle *hinnēh* or *hēn* is also not uncommon at the beginning of refutations to underline Yahweh's coming action, as in Isa 28,16; Ezek 37,12; Isa 49,16 and 49,22. *hēn* is also found in the second verse of a programmatic refutation in Ezek 18,4. The refutation in Jer 8,8 is introduced by *'ākēn hinnēh* which stresses the contrast with the quotation (p.33). Rhetorical questions too emphasise the rejection of the quotation at the beginning of refutations. In Isa 49,15 and Hag 1,4 the programmatic refutation is expressed as a rhetorical question. In Isa 40,28 the refutation begins with a double rhetorical question.

The formula of the recognition of Yahweh takes its place at the end of the refutations in Ezek 11,10.12; 33,29; 37,13 and Isa 49,23. The refutation in Ezek 20,34-44 is punctuated by three such formulae in vv.38.42 and 44. The actions announced by Yahweh which display the falsity of the quotations will lead to a deeper awareness that he indeed is the Lord. The formula *ne'um 'ǎdōnāy yhwh* is also not infrequent to stress various elements of the refutations. It is found particularly in Ezekiel. In Ezek 18,3; 20,33; 33,11 and Isa 49,18 it follows *hay-'ānî*; in the last case it is reduced to *ne'um-yhwh*. In Ezek 12,25.28 and 20,44 the full formula concludes the refutation. It is also found in Ezek 11,8 and 20,40.

The Double Refutation

A particular development of the refutation in the disputation speeches is the double refutation, found not only in Ezek 11,2-12; 11,14-17 and 33,23-29, but also in Isa 49,14-25 and Hag 1,2.4-11.

The reason for defending the presence of two distinct refutations in these

texts is that in all but one case a different argument is used in the two refutations. This separation of two refutations is underlined by the messenger formula which usually introduces the distinct refutations. In the ten refutations in
these five disputation speeches the messenger formula is absent only in Ezek
11,11; Isa 49,16 and Hag 1,9. Only in Hag 1,9-11 is a new argument not apparent
in the second refutation. Here the prophet gives a new refutation in a more excited tone, but virtually repeating the argument of the first refutation in vv.5-8.
He does however give the reason for the plight of the people for the first time
explicitly in v.9b (p.104). The second refutation thus usually provides a new
argument against the quotation. For this reason other disputation speeches
were considered as having only one refutation, albeit in two or three sections.
Ezek 18,5-18 is one refutation, though it is developed in the three stages of the
three generations (p.59). The refutation in Ezek 33,12-16 gives the two cases of
perversion and conversion, but they are parts of the one argument that a man
can change his fate (p.72). In Ezek 20,34-44 the intention of Yahweh to reign
over his people is explained in three stages. This text might have been considered as having a "triple refutation", each part being closed by the formula of
the recognition of Yahweh in vv.38.42 and 44, but the lack of introductory formulae to the separate parts, and above all the unity of the basic argument with
its climax in the second part of the refutation in vv.39-42, counselled seeing the
three parts as one refutation (pp.70).

What is the relationship of the first to the second refutation in the disputation speeches containing a double refutation? Apart from Hag 1, where the
second refutation virtually repeats the first, the other four disputation speeches
display a chronological progression in the two refutations. The first refutation
in Ezek 11,7-10 deals with the contemporary situation when it admits that the
city may well be a pot to protect the leaders for the present, but the second
refutation in vv.11-12 declares that in the future the city will no longer be a pot
to protect them, and they will become meat inside it. *tihyeh* and *tihyû* in v.11
display the chronological change from the first refutation (p.47). In Ezek 11,16
in the first refutation of the words in 11,15 Yahweh declares that he did take
the exiles far off and became a sanctuary for them for a while. But the second
refutation in 11,17 declares his intention to bring them back and give the land
to them (p.51). Again, the difference in verb forms in the two refutations shows
the chronological sequence. Similarly, in Ezek 33,23-29, vv.25-26 considered the
past and present behaviour of the speakers of the quotation, while vv.27-29
spoke of their coming fate (p.80). Here too the verb forms confirm the
chronological progression. The two refutations in Isa 49,16-23 both make promises for the future, but the content shows how here too a chronological
sequence may be proposed. The first refutation in vv.16-21 speaks of the initial
return of Sion's sons. The second refutation in vv.22-23 widens the spectrum to
see the coming of the nations, who accompany Yahweh's people back to Sion.
The first refutation speaks of the more immediate future, when the oppressors

flee (v.17), and Sion is amazed at her sudden change of fortune (v.21).

In two of the disputation speeches with double refutations the quotation of the people is refuted in stages. The first part of the quotation in Ezek 11,3, "we have plenty of time to build up the houses", is never dealt with, but the second part of the quotation, "this is the pot, and we are the meat", is refuted in two stages. The first refutation denies that the leaders are the meat; the second denies that the city is the pot (p.45). In Ezek 11,14-17 the first refutation in v.16 deals with the claim of the people that the exiles "have gone far from Yahweh", whereas the second refutation in v.17 tackles the claim that "it is to us that the land has been given" (p.51). Both refutations in Ezek 33,25-29 show that those left in Jerusalem will not inherit the land, but only the first refutation in vv.25-26 refers to the issue explicitly (p.78). Both refutations in Isa 49,16-23 show how Yahweh has not abandoned his people. And in Hag 1,5-11 both refutations tackle the complete quotation.

The double refutations in Ezek 11,16-17 and 33,25-29 have the particular characteristic that while the first refutation is directed grammatically to those remaining in the land, the supposed speakers of the quotation, the second refutation is directed grammatically to the actual audience, the exiles (p.48; p.78). This phenomenon confirms that it is correct to see two refutations in these speeches.

Are there occasions in which one refutation would suffice to complete the disputation speech? This is true certainly in Hag 1,2.4-11, where vv. 9-11 may reasonably be seen as not essential to the argument, though they add to the urgency of the speech as a whole (p.104). The two refutations are necessary in Ezek 11,2-12; 11,14-17 and 33,23-29 to complete the argument. In Isa 49,14-25 the elaborate structure of the whole disputation speech, with both programmatic and concluding refutations, shows that, while one refutation might suffice to reject the quotation, the composition is certainly a unit (pp.91-92).

The Programmatic and Concluding Refutations

Another particular device used in some refutations is the programmatic refutation, found in Ezek 18,3-4; 20,33; 33,11; Isa 49,15 and Hag 1,4. This element gives a preliminary refutation of the quotation which will be explained in the detailed refutation which follows. It is thus both programmatic and a refutation. It is found precisely in the five disputation speeches with the longest complete refutations. (A word-count shows that the refutation in Ezek 33,12-16, the shortest complete refutation of the five texts concerned, is longer than the complete refutations in Isa 28,16-19 and Ezek 33,25-29, which have the longest complete refutations outside these five texts.) Thus the programmatic refutation has the particular role of giving a quick rejection of the quotation before lengthy explanation begins. The programmatic refutation contains either the oath formula *ḥay-'ānî* followed by *ne'um 'ădōnāy yhwh*, as in the Ezekiel texts, or a rhetorical question, as in Isa 49,15 and Hag 1,4.

In Isa 49,15 the programmatic refutation contains also a reply to the rhetorical question with a conditional sentence articulated by *gam* ... *we* ... The same elements are found in the concluding refutation in vv.24-25. The concluding refutation, of which this is the only example in the disputation speeches, sums up the rejection of the quotation with a new image. Yahweh's reply is further emphasised by the messenger formula in v.25. Yahweh has not abandoned his people, for he is not only more caring than a mother (v.15), but also more mighty than an awe-inspiring hero (vv.24-25) (pp.96-97).

The Rejoinder and Reply

The final elements of the structure of the disputation speech to be considered can be seen as an extension of the prophet's encounter with the people. The rejoinder and reply are found in Ezek 18,19-20 and twice in Ezek 33,17-20.

In Ezek 18,19 the people contest the prophet's teaching with a question, "why does not the son suffer for the guilt of the father?" They are unwilling to accept Ezekiel's teaching, for it means that they can no longer shift responsibility for their plight to their fathers. The reply summarises Ezekiel's teaching in the refutation. The repeated rejoinder in Ezek 33,17.20, "the way of the Lord cannot be fathomed", is of a different tone for the people express not rejection but incredulity (pp. 76-77). In this case it is completely to their advantage to accept the prophet's teaching that conversion can change their present plight. But they find it hard to believe that there is a solution to their situation and they are reluctant to exert themselves. The prophet turns their own rejoinder against them in v.17b and insists that it is in their power to reform so that life can be theirs. When the people again express their misgivings in v.20a the prophet gives the stark reply, "I will judge each one of you according to his deeds". His curt riposte should shake them into understanding and action.

In both texts where the prophet is called upon to defend his words he does not give additional explanation in the replies, but summarises his own teaching from the refutations.

Such are the elements of the disputation speech in the sixteen texts proposed. The basic structure of introduced quotation and refutation allows minor elements to enrich and develop it, particularly the double refutation, the programmatic refutation, and the rejoinder and reply. But throughout its life the genre retains its clear structure with the two principal parts, the quotation and the refutation. Even in Deutero-Isaiah, the genre is easily recognisable.[10] He adopts the double refutation and programmatic refutation found already in Ezekiel, and enriches the genre with the one instance of a concluding refutation.

Three tables display the principal characteristics of the introductions, quotations and refutations; a final table shows the frequency of the particular elements found in some disputation speeches.

Introductions to the Disputation Speeches

	Formula Coming of Word	Form of Main Verb	Statement or Question	Subject described
Isa 28,14-15		'ămartem	statement	X
Jer 8,8		tō'mᵉrû	question	
Jer 31,29		yō'mᵉrû	statement	
Jer 33,23-24	X	dibbᵉrû	question	X
Ezek 11,2-3		'ōmᵉrîm 3rd p.	statement	X
Ezek 11,14-15	X	'āmᵉrû	statement	X
Ezek 12,21-22	X		question	
Ezek 12,26-27	X	'ōmᵉrîm 3rd p.	statement	X
Ezek 18,1-2	X	mōšᵉlîm 2nd p.	question	
Ezek 20,32		'ōmᵉrîm 2nd p.	statement	
Ezek 33,10		'ămartem	statement	
Ezek 33,23-24	X	'ōmᵉrîm 3rd p.	statement	X
Ezek 37,11b		'ōmᵉrîm 3rd p.	statement	
Isa 40,27		tō'mar/tᵉdabbēr	question	(X)
Isa 49,14		wattō'mer	statement	X
Hag 1,2		'āmᵉrû	statement	X

---

[10] In the case of the disputation speech there is no disintegration of form in Deutero-Isaiah. GRESSMANN, "Die literarische Analyse", 295, maintained that in Deutero-Isaiah the fixed forms used by previous prophets disintegrated. Thus also MUILENBURG, *Isaiah 40-66*, 385.

Quotations in the Disputation Speeches

	Number of Clauses	Synonymous Parallel	Logical Link*	Chiastic Layout
Isa 28,15	6	X	X	X
Jer 8,8	2		X	
Jer 31,29	2			
Jer 33,24	2			
Ezek 11,3	3			
Ezek 11,15	2		X	
Ezek 12,22	2		X	
Ezek 12,27	3	X		X
Ezek 18,2	2			
Ezek 20,32	1			
Ezek 33,10	3			
Ezek 33,24	4		X	X
Ezek 37,11b	3			
Isa 40,27	2	X		X
Isa 49,14	2	X		X
Hag 1,2	1			

* as described on p.110.

Refutations in the Disputation Speeches

	Messenger Formula	Oath Formula	First Person Yahweh	Formula Recognition of Yahweh
Isa 28,16-19	X		X	
Jer 8,8-9				
Jer 31,30				
Jer 33,25-26	X		X	
Ezek 11,7-12	X		X	X2
Ezek 11,16-17	X2		X	
Ezek 12,23-25	X		X	
Ezek 12,28	X		X	
Ezek 18,3-18		X	(X)	
Ezek 20,33-44	X	X	X	X3
Ezek 33,11-16		X	X	
Ezek 33,25-29	X2	X	X	X
Ezek 37,12-13	X		X	X
Isa 40,28-31				
Isa 49,15-25	X2	X	X	X
Hag 1,4-11	X		X	

Particular Elements in the Disputation Speeches

	Remark	Double Refutation	Programmatic Refutation	Concluding Refutation	Rejoinder and Reply
Isa 28,14-19					
Jer 8,8-9					
Jer 31,29-30					
Jer 33,23-26	X				
Ezek 11,2-12	X	X			
Ezek 11,14-17		X			
Ezek 12,21-25					
Ezek 12,26-28					
Ezek 18,1-20			X		X
Ezek 20,32-44			X		
Ezek 33,10-20			X		X2
Ezek 33,23-29		X			
Ezek 37,11b-13					
Isa 40,27-31					
Isa 49,14-25		X	X	X	
Hag 1,2.4-11		X	X		

3. The Setting of the Disputation Speech in the life of ancient Israel

The clarification of the structure and aim of the disputation speech should lead to certain conclusions about its setting in the life of Israel. What was the sociological and cultural background of the genre? What were the issues in the context of which the disputation speech was used? The setting is not necessarily derived exclusively from the genre. Other elements beside genre, and not excluding content, can contribute to the description of the setting in life[11]. The search for the setting in life of the disputation speech is above all an attempt to relate the literature to the life and historical situations in which it arose[12].

---

[11] RICHTER, *Exegese*, 146, uses content in the search for the *Sitz im Leben*. LAPOINTE, "Sitz im Leben", 486-487, by way of example, notes that the text of Ps 117 reveals it is a hymnic prayer. But the conclusion that it was used for the celebration of the enthronement of Yahweh, or at the paschal supper, does not come directly from a consideration of genre. Lapointe considers that everything "read between the lines" in the text is pertinent to the *Sitz im Leben*.

[12] BUSS, "Sitz im Leben", 165, sees this elucidation of the relationship of the literature to life as the principal value of the *Sitz im Leben*.

In his study of the disputation speech in Deutero-Isaiah von Waldow proposed that the *Sitz im Leben* of the disputation speech was "everyday life" (*der Alltag*), all those situations where differences of opinion might arise[13]. A more detailed description of the setting should surely be sought. Why did this particular genre reach its peak only comparatively late in the history of prophecy? Were not differences of opinion evident very early on in prophecy?

Historical Setting

The disputation speech is a genre found principally in immediate pre-exilic, exilic and immediate post-exilic Israel. The one exception to these dates is Isa 28,14-19, which is to be set most probably in the reign of Hezekiah, and thus a century earlier than the speeches of Jeremiah[14]. One might consider that Isa 28,14-19 is a tentative and isolated use of the genre, since the quotation is unusually long and explicitly denied in all its parts towards the end of the refutation. Jer 8,8-9 and Jer 31,29-30 with their introductory formulae *'êkâ tō'm^{e}rû* and *lō'-yō'm^{e}rû 'ôd* also belong to the early stages of the genre. Full development with regular use of formulae comes in Jer 33,23-26 and in Ezekiel. Nevertheless, all the disputation speeches, with the exception of Isa 28,14-19, are to be assigned to a specific historical period of approximately a century.

It was during this period that the audience of the prophets reached a peak of scepticism and criticism[15]. The prophets were consequently obliged to seek new techniques to persuade the people with more cogent arguments. The disputation speech can be seen as a particular device designed to confront erroneous opinions directly and convince the people of the prophet's teaching. It is a sign of the vigour with which the prophets tackled their mission in a time of crisis. The prophets are in touch with their people, aware of what is said in their environment and thus able to counter whatever is unacceptable.

Credibility of the Quotations

There is no way of knowing with certainty whether the quotations were actually pronounced by the people, but they are always credible and true to life. Even the quotation given in Isa 28,15 is to be seen not as a caricature of the leaders' words, but as a true to life expression of their attitude. It is an arrogant affirmation of absolute trust in their political prowess and ability to forge agreements which will save them from all danger (pp.26-28). The words

---

[13] Von Waldow, *Anlass und Hintergrund*, 28.
[14] Wildberger, *Jesaja*, 1072.
[15] Von Rad, *Theologie*, II, 272-274.

attributed by Ezekiel to those back in Israel in Ezek 11,3; 11,15; 12,22; 18,2 and 33,24 present a special problem of authenticity. How did Ezekiel know what was being said by those left in the land? One might reasonably consider that there were still contacts between the two groups, but Ezekiel could well have composed these quotations himself in conformity with what he knew of the attitudes of the people in Jerusalem. The rejoinders in Ezek 18,19 and 33,17.20 give an idea of the expected reaction of the people to the prophet's message, reluctance to accept personal guilt in the former case and slowness to grasp the urgency of changing their lives in the latter. Both quotations and rejoinders are always true to life and credible, though their absolute authenticity as quotations of the people must remain an open question. They provide a genuine source of information regarding the ministry of the prophets, describing the problems they had to deal with at this time, and the attitudes they had to face[16].

Problems raised in the Quotations

The setting of the disputation speech is that of difference of opinion between prophets and people. With this genre the prophet confronts the people's mistaken opinions directly. The specific problems concerning which the genre is employed are various, but certain similarities of theme can be detected in the disputation speeches. All the quotations and consequent refutations can be placed in two major groups according to content. In the first group the quotation expresses a fundamental arrogance, trust in personal righteousness and ability to survive, which tends to shift all guilt to others. A second group contains quotations voicing loss of trust in Yahweh and despair due to sin. While in the first group the speakers are answered generally with harsh words, the speakers in the second group receive encouragement from Yahweh.

Arrogance challenged (see the table on p.125)

Within each major group there are disputation speeches tackling similar issues. In Isa 28,14-19 the leaders of the people in Jerusalem express their confidence in their own ability to survive destruction due to their forging of political arrangements and their dishonesty. They boast that they have reached an agreement with Death and Sheol. They thus reject trust in Yahweh and the

---

[16] WOLFF, "Das Zitat", 66-68, gives three possible characteristics of the content which indicate the authenticity of a quotation: it should mirror the historical and cultural background in which it was used; it should fit with the manner of thought and speech of those quoted; and unintelligibility of a quotation is a sign of probable authenticity. The final characteristic does not apply to the quotations in the disputation speeches.

preaching of the prophet (pp.26-27). The refutation explicitly contradicts their words, and announces their coming punishment. A similar arrogance and trust in unscrupulous methods is apparent in Ezek 11,2-12. The leaders of the people after the first deportation are quite sure they will have plenty of time to build up the city, for they regard themselves as the chosen ones, the meat protected by the pot. But the reply again repudiates their confidence. They have trusted in violence to establish themselves. Though for the present they may survive, the time will come when they themselves will perish, and the city will no longer protect them (p.47). In both these disputation speeches it is the leaders' arrogant trust in unscrupulous political methods, including even the murder of opponents, which is attacked. For such conduct they are condemned.

A less aggressive kind of confidence is expressed and refuted in Ezek 12,21-25. The speakers are beginning to despise prophecies of coming doom. They take advantage of the principle laid down in Deut 18,21-22, that prophecies which remain unfulfilled are not of Yahweh, to belittle the words of the prophets. They rely on the words of the Law and feel sure that no calamities will reach them (pp.53-54). Yahweh's prophet rejects their confidence by reiterating that what Yahweh has spoken will soon come to pass. A similar sense of security is expressed in Jer 8,8, where the people consider themselves wise due to their possession of the Law of Yahweh. The reply given here again puts the word spoken by the prophet from Yahweh above the Law. The Law cannot be trusted due to the lies introduced into it by disreputable scribes. It is the words announced by the prophet which must be heeded. The Law is again used by the people in Ezek 18,1-20 and Jer 31,29-30. Relying on the description of God who punishes the sins of the fathers in the children to the third and fourth generation (Exod 34,7; Num 14,18), the people conclude that they are suffering for the sins of others. The calamities falling on Israel are due to previous generations of sinners, they insinuate. While Jer 31,29-30 promises that the time will come when the people will understand God's ways correctly and consequently each recognise his own personal responsibility, Ezek 18,1-20 gives a lengthy justification for the idea that "it is the person who sins that shall die" (v.4). Guilt and punishment do not pass from generation to generation. Once more the word of the prophet shows up an inadequate understanding of the Law of God.

Arrogance, self-confidence and failure to recognise guilt is betrayed in another context when in Ezek 11,14-17 and Ezek 33,23-29 those left in Jerusalem both before and after 587 make their claims to inheritance of the land. In Ezek 11 the claim is based on the fact that the exiles have gone far from Yahweh, morally in sinning against him and physically too due to deportation (p.50). They have lost all rights to the land due to their guilt. They are not expected to return. The refutations show that Yahweh has other ideas. In Ezek 33 those remaining after the destruction of the city consider that they must be specially chosen by Yahweh as Abraham was. They are still blind to their own guilt, but it is brought home to them in vv.25-26, with the punishment deserved in vv.27-29. Both these disputation speeches use "pious" reasons to justify the claims of the quotations. In the former the speakers pass a self-righteous judgement on the exiles, while in the latter they express their esteem for Abraham. As in the four previous disputation speeches, where the Law was used in different ways to justify the people's position, so here a false righteousness is apparent in the words attributed to the people, a righteousness by which neither Yahweh nor his prophet is fooled.

A final disputation speech in which arrogance and failure to recognise personal guilt are confronted is the post-exilic text, Hag 1,2.4-11. In this case the people have already suffered the dire consequences of their neglect of Yahweh and their failure to rebuild his house. The prophet calls on them to consider their situation (vv.5.7), understand the reasons for it, and remedy their plight by beginning work on the temple.

Despair relieved (see the table on p.125)

The quotations in the first major group of disputation speeches betrayed arrogance, self-confidence and failure to recognise personal guilt. A self-righteous tone pervaded them all. They contrast strongly with the quotations in the remaining disputation speeches, which give voice rather to lack of confidence, despair and loss of trust in Yahweh. This can be accompanied by an awareness of guilt, as is quite explicit in Ezek 33,10.

The quotation in Jer 33,24 states that, although Yahweh did indeed choose the two clans of Israel and Judah as his people, he has now rejected them. The speakers, certain elements among the people, consider that Israel and Judah have lost their status as a nation, and are to be despised. The tone of this quotation is not one of genuine despair, as the explanatory remark in v.24b makes clear, and the speakers seem even content to be relieved of the status of being God's chosen people (p.39). With a solemn oath Yahweh repudiates such ideas and affirms his constant commitment to his people.

The disputation speeches which give words of the exiles in Ezekiel voice a more genuine despondency and loss of trust in Yahweh. In Ezek 12,26-28 the exiles express their scepticism that the prophet's predictions of prosperity will be realised in the near future (pp.57-58). As in Ezek 12,21-25, the power of Yahweh's word is affirmed in reply. In Ezek 20,32-44 the people bemoan their destiny as that of serving gods of wood and stone (pp.66-67). Yahweh is unequivocal in his rejection of this vision of their future. They must destroy all idols, for their true destiny is to serve him in the land of Israel. In Ezek 33,10 the speakers express their despair due to a deep awareness of their sinfulness. They are wasting away due to their sins and transgressions. The prophet announces to them the possibility of conversion and the promise of life. It is up to them to grasp the opportunity of life. Only with their effort will they be granted life. By contrast, when in Ezek 37,11b the exiles announce their despair and the extinction of their hopes, Yahweh promises unconditionally that they will be restored to life and return to the land of Israel.

The disputation speeches in Deutero-Isaiah are also intended to encourage the people and to bring a message of consolation to the despondent exiles. To Israel's repeated lament in 40,27, that Yahweh has abandoned his people, the prophet replies with a reminder that Yahweh is the God who created all, the God who does not tire and who strengthens the weary. In Isa 49,14-25 the quotation is a lament of the personified city. Yahweh replies that he has not abandoned, nor forgotten Sion, and gives a detailed description of his plans for the restoration and future prosperity of his people.

The Prophet confronts his People

Thus the disputation speeches fall into two basic groups. Whenever the leaders put their trust absolutely in shameless political machinations (Isa 28,15; Ezek 11,3); whenever the people cling to the Law and fail to heed the word announced by the prophet (Jer 8,8; Ezek 12,22); whenever they consider themselves chosen and guiltless, and shift the guilt to the shoulders of others (Jer 31,29; Ezek 18,2; Ezek 11,15; 33,24); whenever they do not recognise the consequences of neglecting Yahweh (Hag 1,2), then the prophets announce Yahweh's message in harsh and uncompromising terms. The one exception is Ezek 11,16.17, where the refutations announce a bright future for the exiles in reply to the arrogant assertions of those back in the land. When, on the other hand, the people voice despair and despondency about the future (Ezek 12,27; 20,32; 33,10; 37,11b; Isa 40,27; 49,14), or some of the people voice the opinion that Yahweh has indeed abandoned those he chose (Jer 33,24), then the prophets restate Yahweh's commitment to his people and his offer of life.

In the majority of cases the prophet's refutation is delivered directly to the speakers of the quotation. This is not the case in those speeches of Ezekiel where the exiled prophet replies to words attributed to those back in Jerusalem (Ezek 11,2-12; 11,14-17; 12,21-25; 18,1-20 and 33,23-29). The prophet's actual audience is the exiles. But while the prophet's message refutes the words of those in Jerusalem, it is far from irrelevant for the exiles. The words of arrogance of those in Jerusalem are answered by warnings of punishment due to them in Ezek 11,2-12 and 33,23-29. In Ezek 12,21-25 it is announced that the promised disaster will indeed come upon those in Jerusalem. In Ezek 18,1-20 the lesson of each man's accountability must be taken to heart both by the exiles and those left behind. Ezek 11,14-17 is especially relevant to the exiles, for the proud words of those left in Jerusalem are countered by the announcement that it is not they but the exiles who will in fact possess the land.

Thus in all the disputation speeches the prophets use words heard from the people or credibly attributed to the people as a starting-point in confronting their audience, who are usually the very speakers of the quotations, and correct their mistaken ideas. The prophets must teach their audience to understand God's demands correctly and lead them to a true trust in Yahweh. Both the disputation speeches which announce the danger of punishment to arrogant speakers and those which promise help to the despairing are found in times of crisis. It was the radical nature and urgency of these challenges to God by the people which led the prophets to use this genre to confront the people directly. When the people trust only in themselves and abandon their trust in Yahweh the prophet must do all he can to change their minds.

Among the prophets the disputation speech had a brief life. There is no evidence of its use after Haggai. It declined with the decline of prophecy. But a later prophet who desired to lead his disciples and the people from their inadequate opinions to a deeper awareness of the demands of God's Law was to use a form of speech with striking similarities to the prophetic disputation speech.

4. Disputation Speeches of the prophet Jesus?

Early in this study a distinction was drawn between the "disputation" and the "disputation speech". While the former reports a controversy in direct speech, in the latter the prophet first quotes the opinion of the people and then goes on to refute it (pp.9-10). In the disputation speech the prophet alone speaks. Reference was made at that early stage to the disputations between Jesus and his adversaries in the NT (often given the designation *Streitgespräch*). The genre and function of the disputation speech have been clarified by an examination of the prophetic disputation speeches in the OT. The disputation speech had a short life. But were those the only uses of the genre?

Recent investigation of the "antitheses" in Matt 5,21-48 has dealt with the question of the traditional or redactional nature of the six original sections found in vv.21-22.27-28.31-32.33-37.38-42.43-48[17]. In connection with this issue NT scholars have attempted to explain the origin of the form used here.

Each antithesis has a basic two-part structure. The first antithesis, vv.21-22, is given here as an example:

---

[17] Both Lohse, "Ich aber", 189, and Guelich, "The Antitheses", 445, who have made particular studies of the form of the antitheses, consider vv.23-26 and vv.29-30 to be additional to the original speeches.

Problems raised in the Quotations

Isa 28,14-19		political	
Ezek 11,2-12			
Jer 8,8-9	arrogance	false righteousness due to	Law
Ezek 12,21-25			
Jer 31,29-30			
Ezek 18,1-20			
Ezek 11,14-17			exiles' sin — guilt shifted to others
Ezek 33,23-29			God's choice
Hag 1,2.4-11		neglect of Yahweh	
Jer 33,23-26		sham despair of a group	
Isa 40,12-31	despair	genuine despair of exiles	Yahweh has abandoned his people
Isa 49,14-25			
Ezek 12,26-28			prophecies for future
Ezek 20,32-44			people to serve idols
Ezek 33,10-20			people destined for death
Ezek 37,11b-13			

21   You have heard that it was said
        to the men of old:
        You shall not kill,
        and anyone who kills
        shall be liable to judgement.
22   But I say to you:
        Anyone who is angry with his brother
        shall be liable to judgement.
        And anyone who says to his brother "Fool!"
        shall be liable to judgement by the Sanhedrin.
        And anyone who says to his brother "Idiot!"
        shall be liable to the hell of fire.

This first antithesis gives the full structure of the form found here. The introduction "you have heard that it was said to the men of old" is the complete formula, as found again in v.33. An abbreviated version, "you have heard that it was said", is used in vv.27.38 and 43. V.31 simply has "again it was said". After this follows the quotation of what has been handed down from the "men of old". The quotation is usually either a citation from the Law, or a paraphrase from it[18]. In two cases the material is developed. Matt 5,21 develops Exod 20,13 and Deut 5,17 with the words "anyone who kills shall be liable to judgement", and v.43 develops Lev 19,18 with "you shall hate your enemy"[19]. After the words based on the Law the introduction to Jesus' reply, constant in all six antitheses, reads "But I say to you". Jesus' replies can be seen either as making the Law more radical, as in v.22, where the command forbidding murder becomes more far-reaching, or as contradicting the words handed down, as in v.32, where Jesus rejects divorce[20].

Such is the form of the antitheses investigated by NT scholars. D. Daube proposed that Jesus adapted for his use a form employed by the rabbis in midrashic explanations of the meaning of biblical texts. The rabbinical form begins with "I might understand" (šwmᶜ 'ny). Daube gives an example from the Mekilta on Exod 20,12[21]. The second part of the rabbinical form contains the

---

[18] Matt 5,27 contains a direct quotation of Exod 20,14 and Deut 5,18. Matt 5,38 quotes Exod 21,24; Lev 24,20 and Deut 19,21. Matt 5,31 contains material from Deut 24,1. Matt 5,33 can be traced to Lev 19,12; Num 30,3 and Deut 23,22.

[19] DAUBE, "Ye have heard", 56, n. 2.

[20] LOHSE, "Ich aber", 189-190, and GUELICH, "The Antitheses", 445, consider the antitheses regarding murder, adultery and oath-taking (vv.22.28.34-37) as radicalisations of the Law, while those concerning divorce, the talion and love (vv.32.39-42.44-48) are seen as contradicting the tradition. JEREMIAS, Theologie, 241, and MEIER, Law and History, 134-135, divide the antitheses differently. They regard the antithesis on oath-taking (vv.34-37) as an abrogation of the Law, and they see the command on love (vv.44-48) as a radicalisation.

[21] DAUBE, "Ye have heard", 55. A similar rendering of šwmᶜ 'ny is given by LAUTERBACH, Mekilta de-Rabbi Ishmael, II, 257.

verb *'MR*. Matthew adapts the formulae to achieve "Ye might understand literally" and "But I say to you!"[22]. The rabbinical form was used to give a fuller interpretation and reject a narrow one. But in the adapted form Jesus lays down the real demand of the Law against a literal interpretation. Daube considers the two forms to be similar; the gulf between them is not great. Jesus is the upholder of the Law who gives a proper interpretation, like the rabbis, but with his own supreme authority[23].

Daube's explanation of the origin of the form of the antitheses has not gone unchallenged. E. Lohse has maintained that Jesus' use of the form is fundamentally different from the rabbis', for Jesus does not challenge a possible interpretation of the Law, but an actual command entrusted to the listeners[24]. Lohse tracks down the phrase "But I say to you" *(w'ny 'wmr)* in Tannaitic discussions, especially in the Tosefta, where views differing from the norm of the Mishnah are expressed[25]. There are also similarities of content between Jesus' teaching and contemporary Jewish interpretations of the Law. But Jesus' antitheses are fundamentally different in taking a position against what was received as tradition, what was "said to the men of old", not against some possible misinterpretation[26].

R. Guelich follows Lohse's lead. He admits the parallels in the use of formulae, and that the radical content of the antitheses has some parallels with Qumran and the teaching of certain rabbis. But there are in fact no parallels to the antitheses as a whole. No-one before Jesus proposed his interpretation of the Law in contrast to what was "said to the men of old". Guelich reaches the conclusion that the form has its origin in Jesus' ministry. He regards the first, second and fourth antitheses as coming to Matthew from the tradition, while Matthew adapted the material in the three others, which have parallels in Luke, to this form. The setting of the antitheses is Jesus' encounter with the "righteous". Jesus announces God's radical demands which challenge those who jealously defend the letter of the Law. The form has its origin, in Guelich's view, in the ministry of Jesus and in his totally new approach to the Law[27].

But is the form of the antitheses totally new? Cannot the disputation speech shed some light on the form used here? Can the antitheses be seen as disputation speeches of the prophet Jesus?

The similarities between the antitheses and the prophetic disputation speeches are many. The antitheses show the basic two-part structure preceded by a formal introduction. The introductions invariably contain the verb *errethē*,

---

[22] DAUBE, "Ye have heard", 55-58.
[23] DAUBE, "Ye have heard", 58-60.
[24] LOHSE, "Ich aber", 192-193.
[25] LOHSE, "Ich aber", 193-195. He gives the example of Tosefta Soṭa VI, 6-11. An English rendering can be found in NEUSNER, *Tosefta* Third Division, 172-176.
[26] LOHSE, "Ich aber", 196-198.
[27] GUELICH, "The Antitheses", 455-457.

providing an equivalent to the forms of 'MR found in every disputation speech (p.108). The introduction leads in what might be described as an opinion of the people derived from the Law. This quotation is then challenged in the second part. A new approach to the command is announced, which is either a radicalisation or an abrogation of the tradition. As in the prophetic disputation speech, a formally introduced quotation of the people is challenged.

But there are differences. The "quotation" is taken from the Law, and is hardly a saying from the lips of the people, or even attributed to them. But the quotation does express their opinion, in so far as it gives expression to the legal traditions accepted by them and by which their lives were regulated. One might then hesitate to call Jesus' replies refutations. Where his reply amounts to a contradiction of the Law, one might acceptably speak of a refutation, but this is not so easy in the antitheses where Jesus' reply leads to a radicalisation of the command. Nevertheless, in each antithesis, an accepted tenet of the Law is redefined, altered, corrected and so to some degree the old way of thinking is refuted. The command "you shall not kill" is not refuted in 5,22, but the thinking behind it which might infer that anything less than killing was acceptable is indeed rejected.

The antitheses in Matt 5,21-48 can well be seen as disputation speeches. It is above all their formal structure which shows that they can be regarded thus. The structure reveals the function of correcting the people's opinions, the function of all prophetic disputation speeches. Jesus' aim in announcing the antitheses is to correct inadequate or false ideas of God's Law, to deepen the people's understanding of his will for his people. His aim in these six sections might be compared to that of the prophet in the disputation speech Jer 8,8-9. The aim is that the people should rely not on the possession of the Law for their security and wisdom, but rather that they should constantly listen to the word of the prophet of God. The antitheses have a similar aim to those disputation speeches which set out to correct an unacceptable interpretation of the Law, Jer 31,29-30; Ezek 12,21-25 and 18,1-20[28].

Jesus uses the prophetic genre of disputation speech to teach his hearers and correct their poor grasp of God's demands. The really original element in the antitheses comes at the beginning of the refutations. So often in the OT disputation speeches the refutations began with the messenger formula, "thus says the Lord" (pp.111-112). In Jesus' disputation speeches the formula is always "But I say to you". Jesus, with the supreme authority vested in him by

---

[28] Matt 5 contains the only disputation speeches in the Gospels. But a case can surely be made for seeing Jas 4,13-17 as a disputation speech. The introduction and quotation in v.13 are followed by vv.14-17, a refutation without formal introduction. A particular parallel to Ezek 12,23 is found in the new quotation in v.15, which forms part of the refutation. The theme of the quotation in Jas 4,13 is not unlike that in Ezek 11,3, in that confidence in future prosperity implies scant regard for God. The refutation in Jas 4,14-17, however, has a moralising tone, rather than announcing a violent end for the speakers of the quotation.

the Father, announces his challenge to the Law with the authority of God himself. The formula "But I say to you" looks back critically to what the people hold, and opens the way for the words which come from God. The formula sums up the aim of the prophetic disputation speech, to convert the minds and hearts of the people, to lead them from their inadequate ideas to true faith in God. The genre was used in the OT in times of crisis. With the prophet Jesus it is a genre of the *kairos*, the crisis of the irruption of God's kingdom into the world.

The disputation speech is a direct encounter of God's messenger, the prophet, with the people, an encounter in which the prophet meets the people where they stand. In the disputation speech God's word confronts the inadequacies of man's opinions. The prophet's word comes to transform the hearts of the people, to lead them to an awareness of their guilt and to a secure trust in God. When Jesus uses the disputation speech he too endeavours to change men's hearts, to lead them from where they stand to a deeper knowledge of his Father's will.

Bibliography

ACKROYD P. R., *Exile and Restoration*. A Study of Hebrew Thought of the Sixth Century BC (Old Testament Library; London 1968).

ALONSO SCHOEKEL L., *Estudios de Poética Hebrea* (Barcelona 1963).

ALONSO SCHOEKEL L., SICRE DÍAZ J. L., *Profetas*, Comentario I, II (Madrid 1980).

AMSLER S., *Aggée Zacharie 1-8* (CAT XIc; Neuchâtel-Paris 1981).

AUVRAY P., "Le Prophète comme Guetteur. Ez XXXIII,1-20", *RB* 71 (1964) 191-205.

BALLA E., "Amos", *RGG* I (²1927) 306-309.

BALTZER D., *Ezechiel und Deuterojesaja*. Berührungen in der Heilserwartung der beiden grossen Exilspropheten (BZAW 121; Berlin 1971).

BARTH H., *Die Jesaja-Worte in der Josiazeit*. Israel und Assur als Thema einer produktiven Neuinterpretation der Jesajaüberlieferung (WMANT 48; Neukirchen 1977).

BARTH H., STECK O. H., *Exegese des Alten Testaments*. Leitfaden der Methodik (Neukirchen ⁸1978).

BARTH J., "שׁוֹט שֵׁטֶף", *ZAW* 33 (1913) 306-307.

BEGRICH J., *Studien zu Deuterojesaja* (BWANT, Vierte Folge, 25; Stuttgart 1938).

BENTZEN A., *Introduction to the Old Testament* (Copenhagen ⁷1967).

BERTHOLET A., *Hesekiel* (HAT 13; Tübingen 1936).

BEUKEN W. A. M., *Haggai - Sacharja 1-8*. Studien zur Überlieferungsgeschichte der frühnachexilischen Prophetie (Studia Semitica Neerlandica 10; Assen 1967).

BLACK M., "Scribe", *IDB* IV (1962) 246-248.

BOECKER H. J., "Bemerkungen zur formgeschichtlichen Terminologie des Buches Maleachi", *ZAW* 78 (1966) 78-80.

BOEHMER S., *Heimkehr und neuer Bund*. Studien zu Jeremia 30-31 (Göttinger Theologische Arbeiten 5; Göttingen 1976).

BOER P. A. H., "Einige Bemerkungen und Gedanken zum Lied in 1. Samuel 2,1-10", *Beiträge zur Alttestamentlichen Theologie* (FS. W. Zimmerli; Hrsg. H. DONNER, R. HANHART, R. SMEND) (Göttingen 1977) 53-59.

BONNARD P.-E., *Le Second Isaïe*. Son Disciple et leurs Editeurs (EBib; Paris 1972).

BRIGHT J., *Jeremiah* (AB 21; New York 1965).

BROCKELMANN C., *Hebräische Syntax* (Neukirchen 1956).

BUSS M. J., "The Idea of Sitz im Leben — History and Critique", *ZAW* 90 (1978) 157-170.

CARROLL R. P., *From Chaos to Covenant*. Uses of Prophecy in the Book of Jeremiah (London 1981).

CHILDS B. S., *Isaiah and the Assyrian Crisis* (SBT II,3; London 1967).

CLIFFORD R. J., "The Function of Idol Passages in Second Isaiah", *CBQ* 42 (1980) 450-464.

CODY A., "When is the Chosen People called a Gôy?", *VT* 14 (1964) 1-6.

CONRAD E. W., "Second Isaiah and the Priestly Oracle of Salvation", *ZAW* 93 (1981) 234-246.

COOKE G. A., *The Book of Ezekiel* (ICC; Edinburgh 1936).

CORNILL C. H., *Das Buch Jeremia* (Leipzig 1905).

DAHOOD M., *Psalms* II (AB 17; New York ²1973).

——, "Ugaritic-Hebrew Parallel Pairs", *Ras Shamra Parallels*. The Texts from Ugarit and the Hebrew Bible III (ed. S. Rummel) (AnOr 51; Roma 1981) 1-206.

Daube D., "Ye have heard — but I say unto you", *The New Testament and Rabbinic Judaism* (Jordan Lectures 1952; London 1956) 55-62.

Del Olmo Lete G., "Estructura literaria de Ez. 33,1-20", *EstBib* 22 (1963) 5-31.

Dietrich W., *Jesaja und die Politik* (BEvT 74; München 1976).

Duhm B., *Das Buch Jeremia* (Kurzer Hand-Commentar zum Alten Testament XI; Tübingen-Leipzig 1901).

——, *Das Buch Jesaia* (HKAT III/1; Göttingen ²1902).

Eichrodt W., *Theologie des Alten Testaments* I (Göttingen ⁵1957).

——, *Der Prophet Hesekiel* (ATD 22; Göttingen 1966).

Eissfeldt O., "Schwerterschlagene bei Hesekiel", *Studies in Old Testament Prophecy* (presented to T. H. Robinson; ed. H. H. Rowley) (Edinburgh 1950) 73-81.

——, *Einleitung in das Alte Testament* (Tübingen ³1964).

——, "Jahwe Zebaoth", *Kleine Schriften* III (Tübingen 1966) 103-123.

Elliger K., *Das Buch der zwölf kleinen Propheten* II (ATD 25; Göttingen ⁷1975).

——, *Deuterojesaja* (BKAT XI/1; Neukirchen-Vluyn 1978).

Exum J. C., "Isaiah 28-32: A Literary Approach", *Society of Biblical Literature 1979 Seminar Papers* II (ed. P. J. Achtemeier) (Missoula 1979) 123-151.

Fischer J. A., "Notes on the Literary Form and Message of Malachi", *CBQ* 34 (1972) 315-320.

Fohrer G., *Ezechiel* (HAT 13; Tübingen 1955).

——, *Das Alte Testament.* Einführung in Bibelkunde und Literatur des Alten Testaments und in Geschichte und Religion Israels, Zweiter und dritter Teil (Gütersloh 1970).

Fuhs H. F., *Sehen und Schauen.* Die Wurzel *ḥzh* im Alten Orient und im Alten Testament. Ein Beitrag zum prophetischen Offenbarungsempfang (FzB 32; Würzburg 1978).

Garscha J., *Studien zum Ezechielbuch.* Eine redaktionskritische Untersuchung von Ez 1-39 (Europäische Hochschulschriften XXIII/23; Frankfurt 1974).

Gerleman G., "*rṣh*, Gefallen haben", *THAT* II (²1979) 810-813.

Gerstenberger E., "*ḥsh*, sich bergen", *THAT* I (³1978) 621-623.

——, "*tᶜb* pi., verabscheuen", *THAT* II (²1979) 1051-1055.

Gese H., "Die strömende Geissel des Hadad und Jesaja 28,15 und 18", *Archäologie und Altes Testament* (FS. K. Galling; Hrsg. A. Kuschke, E. Kutsch) (Tübingen 1970) 127-134.

Giesebrecht F., *Das Buch Jeremia* (HKAT III/2/1; Göttingen 1907).

Gitay Y., *Prophecy and Persuasion.* A Study of Isaiah 40-48 (Forum Theologiae Linguisticae 14; Bonn 1981).

Graffy A., "The Literary Genre of Isaiah 5,1-7", *Bib* 60 (1979) 400-409.

Gressmann H., *Die älteste Geschichtsschreibung und Prophetie Israels* (von Samuel bis Amos und Hosea) (Die Schriften des Alten Testaments II/I; Göttingen 1910).

——, "Die literarische Analyse Deuterojesajas", *ZAW* 34 (1914) 254-297.

——, *Der Messias* (FRLANT 43 [Neue Folge 26]; Göttingen 1929).

Guelich R., "The Antitheses of Matthew V.21-48: Traditional and/or Redactional?", *NTS* 22 (1975-1976) 444-457.

Gunkel H., "Propheten: II. Seit Amos", *RGG* IV (¹1913) 1866-1886.

——, "Die Propheten als Schriftsteller und Dichter", in H. Schmidt, *Die grossen Propheten* (Die Schriften des Alten Testaments II/II; Göttingen 1915) xxxvi-lxxii.

——, "Propheten: IIB. Propheten Israels seit Amos", *RGG* IV (²1930) 1538-1554.

Hardmeier C., *Texttheorie und biblische Exegese.* Zur rhetorischen Funktion der Trauermetaphorik in der Prophetie (BEvT 79; München 1978).

Hermisson H.-J., "Diskussionsworte bei Deuterojesaja. Zur theologischen Argumentation des Propheten", *EvT* 31 (1971) 665-680.

Herntrich V., *Ezechielprobleme* (BZAW 61; Giessen 1933).

HERRMANN J., *Ezechiel* (KAT XI; Leipzig 1924).

HERTZBERG H. W., *Die Samuelbücher* (ATD 10; Göttingen ²1960).

HILLERS D. R., *Treaty-Curses and the Old Testament Prophets* (BibOr 16; Roma 1964).

HOEFFKEN P., "Beobachtungen zu Ezechiel XXXVII, 1-10", *VT* 31 (1981) 305-317.

HOELSCHER G., *Hesekiel*. Der Dichter und das Buch. Eine literarkritische Untersuchung (BZAW 39; Giessen 1924).

HOLLADAY W. L., *The Architecture of Jeremiah 1-20* (Lewisburg 1976).

HORST F., "Exilsgemeinde und Jerusalem in Ez VIII-XI", *VT* 3 (1953) 337-360.

HORST F., ROBINSON T. H., *Die zwölf kleinen Propheten* (HAT 14; Tübingen ³1964).

HOSSFELD F. L., MEYER I., *Prophet gegen Prophet*. Eine Analyse der alttestamentlichen Texte zum Thema: wahre und falsche Propheten (BibB 9; Fribourg 1973).

HOSSFELD F. L., *Untersuchungen zu Komposition und Theologie des Ezechielbuches* (FzB 20; Würzburg 1977).

HUBER F., *Jahwe, Juda und die anderen Völker beim Propheten Jesaja* (BZAW 137; Berlin 1976).

HULST A. R., "ʿam/gōj, Volk", *THAT* II (²1979) 290-325.

HYATT J. P., "Torah in the Book of Jeremiah", *JBL* 60 (1941) 381-396.

IRWIN W. H., *Isaiah 28-33*. Translation with Philological Notes (BibOr 30; Rome 1977).

JENNI E., "jōm, Tag", *THAT* I (³1978) 707-726.

——, "ʿōlām, Ewigkeit", *THAT* II (²1979) 228-243.

JEPSEN A., "ʾāman", *TWAT* I (1973) 313-348.

JEREMIAS J., *Neutestamentliche Theologie*. Erster Teil: Die Verkündigung Jesu (Gütersloh 1971).

JONGELING B., "Lākēn dans l'Ancien Testament", *Remembering All the Way ...* (uitgegeven door A. S. VAN DER WOUDE) (OTS XXI; Leiden 1981) 190-200.

JOÜON P., *Grammaire de l'Hébreu Biblique* (Rome 1923).

KAISER O., *Der Prophet Jesaja*. Kapitel 13-39 (ATD 18; Göttingen 1973).

——, *Einleitung in das Alte Testament*. Einführung in ihre Ergebnisse und Probleme (Gütersloh ⁴1978).

KAISER O., KUEMMEL W. G., ADAM G., *Einführung in die exegetischen Methoden* (München ⁵1975).

KLOPFENSTEIN M. A., *Die Lüge nach dem Alten Testament*. Ihr Begriff, ihre Bedeutung und ihre Beurteilung (Zürich 1964).

KNIERIM R., "Old Testament Form Criticism Reconsidered", *Int* 27 (1973) 435-468.

KNIGHT G. A. F., *Deutero-Isaiah*. A Theological Commentary on Isaiah 40-55 (New York-Nashville 1965).

KOCH K., "Haggais unreines Volk", *ZAW* 79 (1967) 52-66.

——, *Was ist Formgeschichte?* Methoden der Bibelexegese (Neukirchen ³1974).

KOCH K. und Mitarbeiter, *Amos* untersucht mit den Methoden einer strukturalen Formgeschichte (AOAT 30; Kevelaer-Neukirchen-Vluyn 1976).

KOEHLER L., *Deuterojesaja stilkritisch untersucht* (BZAW 37; Giessen 1923).

KUEHLEWEIN J., "sēfær, Buch", *THAT* II (²1979) 162-173.

KUHL C., "Die 'Wiederaufnahme' — ein literarkritisches Prinzip?", *ZAW* 64 (1952) 1-11.

KUTSCH E., *Verheissung und Gesetz*. Untersuchungen zum sogenannten "Bund" im Alten Testament (BZAW 131; Berlin 1973).

LAPOINTE R., "La valeur linguistique du Sitz im Leben", *Bib* 52 (1971) 469-487.

LAUTERBACH J. Z. (ed.), *Mekilta de-Rabbi Ishmael* II (Philadelphia 1933).

LOHSE E., "Ich aber sage euch", *Der Ruf Jesu und die Antwort der Gemeinde* (FS. J. Jeremias; Hrsg. E. LOHSE, C. BURCHARD, B. SCHALLER) (Göttingen 1970) 189-203.

LUNDBOM J. R., *Jeremiah: A Study in Ancient Hebrew Rhetoric* (SBLDS 18; Missoula 1975).

McCARTER P. K., *I Samuel* (AB 8; New York 1980).

McKANE W., *Proverbs*. A New Approach (Old Testament Library; London 1970).

McKenzie J. L., *Second Isaiah* (AB 20; New York 1968).

March W. E., "Prophecy", *Old Testament Form Criticism* (ed. J. H. Hayes) (San Antonio 1974) 141-177.

Markert L., *Struktur und Bezeichnung des Scheltworts*. Eine gattungskritische Studie anhand des Amosbuches (BZAW 140; Berlin 1977).

Meier J. P., *Law and History in Matthew's Gospel*. A Redactional Study of Mt. 5:17-48 (AnBib 71; Roma 1976).

Melugin R. F., "Deutero-Isaiah and Form Criticism", *VT* 21 (1971) 326-337.

——, "The Conventional and the Creative in Isaiah's Judgment Oracles", *CBQ* 36 (1974) 301-311.

——, *The Formation of Isaiah 40-55* (BZAW 141; Berlin 1976).

Merendino R. P., *Der Erste und der Letzte*. Eine Untersuchung von Jes 40-48 (VTS 31; Leiden 1981).

——, "Jes 49,14-26: Jahwes Bekenntnis zu Sion und die neue Heilszeit", *RB* 89 (1982) 321-369.

Monloubou L., "Les Genres Prophétiques", *Introduction Critique à l'Ancien Testament* (Introduction à la Bible, Edition Nouvelle, Tome II) (éd. H. Cazelles; Paris 1973) 350-355.

Muilenburg J., *Isaiah 40-66* (IB 5; New York 1956) 381-773.

Muñoz Iglesias S., *Los Géneros Literarios y la Interpretación de la Biblia* (Madrid 1968).

Murphy R. E., *Wisdom Literature: Job, Proverbs, Ruth, Canticles, Ecclesiastes, Esther* (The Forms of the Old Testament Literature 13; Grand Rapids 1981).

Naidoff B. D., "The Rhetoric of Encouragement in Isaiah 40,12-31: A Form-Critical Study", *ZAW* 93 (1981) 62-76.

——, "The Two-fold Structure of Isaiah 45,9-13", *VT* 31 (1981) 180-185.

Neusner J. (ed.), *The Tosefta*. Third Division: Nashim (The Order of Women) (New York 1979).

North C. R., *The Second Isaiah* (Oxford 1964).

Ohler A., *Gattungen im AT*. Ein biblisches Arbeitsbuch, Band 2 (Düsseldorf 1973).

Ottosson M., "$g^e b\hat{u}l$", *TWAT* I (1973) 896-901.

Overholt T. W., *The Threat of Falsehood*. A Study in the Theology of the Book of Jeremiah (SBT II,16; London 1970).

Peter F., "Zu Haggai 1,9", *TZ* 7 (1951) 150-151.

Petersen D. L., "Isaiah 28, A Redaction Critical Study", *Society of Biblical Literature 1979 Seminar Papers* II (ed. P. J. Achtemeier) (Missoula 1979) 101-122.

Pfeiffer E., "Die Disputationsworte im Buche Maleachi. Ein Beitrag zur formgeschichtlichen Struktur", *EvT* 19 (1959) 546-568.

Porteous N. W., "Jerusalem-Zion: The Growth of a Symbol", *Verbannung und Heimkehr*. Beiträge zur Geschichte und Theologie Israels im 6. und 5. Jahrhundert v. Chr. (FS. W. Rudolph; Hrsg. A. Kuschke) (Tübingen 1961) 235-252.

Poznański S., "Zu שׁוֹט שֹׁטֵף", *ZAW* 36 (1916) 119-120.

Procksch O., *Jesaia I* (KAT IX/1; Leipzig 1930).

Ramlot L., "Les moyens d'expression des Prophètes", *DBSup* VIII (1972) 943-973.

Reicke B., "Streitgespräch", *Biblisch-Historisches Handwörterbuch* III (Hrsg. B. Reicke, L. Rost) (Göttingen 1966) 1883-1884.

Reventlow H. G., *Wächter über Israel*. Ezechiel und seine Tradition (BZAW 82; Berlin 1962).

Richter W., *Exegese als Literaturwissenschaft*. Entwurf einer alttestamentlichen Literaturtheorie und Methodologie (Göttingen 1971).

Rudolph W., *Jeremia* (HAT 12; Tübingen ³1968).

——, *Haggai Sacharja 1-8 Sacharja 9-14 Maleachi* (KAT XIII/4; Gütersloh 1976).

Scharbert J., *Solidarität in Segen und Fluch im Alten Testament und in seiner Umwelt* I

(BBB 14; Bonn 1958).

SCHMIDT H., *Die grossen Propheten* (Die Schriften des Alten Testaments II/II; Göttingen 1915).

SCHMIDT W. H., *Einführung in das Alte Testament* (Berlin ²1982).

SCHONEVELD J., "Jeremia XXXI 29,30", *VT* 13 (1963) 339-341.

SCHOORS A., *I am God your Saviour*. A Form-Critical Study of the Main Genres in Is XL-LV (VTS 24; Leiden 1973).

SCHREINER J., "Formen und Gattungen im Alten Testament", *Einführung in die Methoden der biblischen Exegese* (Hrsg. J. SCHREINER) (Würzburg 1971).

SCHULZ H., *Das Todesrecht im Alten Testament*. Studien zur Rechtsform der Mot-Jumat-Sätze (BZAW 114; Berlin 1969).

SCOTT R. B. Y., *Proverbs Ecclesiastes* (AB 18; New York 1965).

SEEBASS H., "*bôš*", *TWAT* I (1973) 568-580.

SELLIN E., FOHRER G., *Einleitung in das Alte Testament* (Heidelberg ¹¹1969).

SIMIAN H., *Die theologische Nachgeschichte der Prophetie Ezechiels*. Form- und traditions- kritische Untersuchung zu Ez 6; 35; 36 (FzB 14; Würzburg 1974).

SPYKERBOER H. C., *The Structure and Composition of Deutero-Isaiah* with special reference to the Polemics against Idolatry (Groningen 1976).

STECK O. H., "Zu Haggai 1,2-11", *ZAW* 83 (1971) 355-379.

STOEBE H. J., *Das erste Buch Samuelis* (KAT VIII/1; Gütersloh 1973).

STOLZ F., "*bōš*, zuschanden werden", *THAT* I (³1978) 269-272.

——, *Das erste und zweite Buch Samuel* (Zürcher Bibelkommentare: Altes Testament 9; Zürich 1981).

TOURNAY R., "Le cantique d'Anne 1 Samuel II,1-10", *Mélanges Dominique Barthélemy* (éd. P. CASETTI, O. KEEL, A. SCHENKER) (OBO 38; Fribourg-Göttingen 1981) 553-576.

TSEVAT M., "*bḥn*", *TWAT* I (1973) 588-592.

TUCKER G. M., *Form Criticism of the Old Testament* (Guides to Biblical Scholarship; Philadelphia 1971).

——, "Form Criticism, OT", *IDBSup* (1976) 342-345.

VAN DER WOUDE A. S., "Micah in Dispute with the Pseudo-Prophets", *VT* 19 (1969) 244-260.

——, "*ṣābā'*, Heer", *THAT* II (²1979) 498-507.

VERMEYLEN J., *Du Prophète Isaïe à l'Apocalyptique*. Isaïe, I-XXXV, miroir d'un demi-millénaire d'expérience religieuse en Israël, Tome I (EBib; Paris 1977).

VETTER D., "*r'h*, sehen", *THAT* II (²1979) 692-701.

VOLZ P., *Der Prophet Jeremia* (KAT X; Leipzig 1922).

——, *Jesaia II* (KAT IX/2; Leipzig 1932).

VON RAD G., *Theologie des Alten Testaments* I (München ⁴1962).

——, *Theologie des Alten Testaments* II (München ⁴1965).

VON WALDOW H.-E., *Anlass und Hintergrund der Verkündigung des Deuterojesaja*. Disser-tation (Bonn 1953).

WALLIS G., "Wesen und Struktur der Botschaft Maleachis", *Das Ferne und Nahe Wort* (FS. L. Rost; Hrsg. F. MAASS) (BZAW 105; Berlin 1967) 229-237.

WEHMEIER G., "*str* hi., verbergen", *THAT* II (²1979) 173-181.

WEISER A., *Das Buch Jeremia* (ATD 20 [Kapitel 1-25,14]; Göttingen ⁷1976) (ATD 21 [Kapitel 25,15-52,34]; Göttingen ⁴1966).

WESTERMANN C., "Sprache und Struktur der Prophetie Deuterojesajas", *Forschung am Alten Testament*. Gesammelte Studien (TBü 24; München 1964) 92-170.

——, *Das Buch Jesaja*. Kapitel 40-66 (ATD 19; Göttingen 1966).

——, "Streitgespräch", *Biblisch-Historisches Handwörterbuch* III (Hrsg. B. REICKE, L. ROST) (Göttingen 1966) 1883.

——, Rezension BEUKEN W. A. M., *Haggai Sacharja 1-8*. Studien zur Überlieferungsgesch-ichte der frühnachexilischen Prophetie (Studia Semitica Neerlandica 10; Assen 1967),

TLZ 94 (1969) 424-426.

——. *Grundformen Prophetischer Rede* (BEvT 31; München ⁵1978).

——, *Der Aufbau des Buches Hiob* (Calwer Theologische Monographien A/6; Stuttgart ³1978).

——, "*kbd*, schwer sein", *THAT* I (³1978) 794-812.

WEVERS J. W., *Ezekiel* (The Century Bible; London 1969).

WHYBRAY R. N., *Isaiah 40-66* (New Century Bible Commentary; London-Grand Rapids 1975).

WILDBERGER H., *Jesaja* (BKAT X/1 [Kapitel 1-12]; Neukirchen-Vluyn ²1980) (BKAT X/3 [Kapitel 28-39]; Neukirchen-Vluyn 1978-1981).

WILSON R. R., "Form-Critical Investigation of the Prophetic Literature: The Present Situation", *Society of Biblical Literature 1973 Seminar Papers* I (ed. G. MACRAE) (Cambridge, Massachusetts 1973) 100-127.

WOLFF H. W., "Das Zitat im Prophetenspruch. Eine Studie zur prophetischen Verkündigungsweise", *Gesammelte Studien zum Alten Testament* (TBü 22; München ²1973) 36-129.

——, *Dodekapropheton 2: Joel und Amos* (BKAT XIV/2; Neukirchen-Vluyn ²1975).

——, *Dodekapropheton 1: Hosea* (BKAT XIV/1; Neukirchen-Vluyn ³1976).

ZIMMERLI W., *Ezechiel* (BKAT XIII/1 [Kapitel 1-24]; Neukirchen-Vluyn ²1979) (BKAT XIII/2 [Kapitel 25-48]; Neukirchen-Vluyn ²1979).

Index of Scripture References

Index of Authors